GREAT GUNFIGHTERS
OF THE WEST

by
CARL W. BREIHAN

The Naylor Company
Book Publishers of the Southwest
San Antonio, Texas

Other books by Carl W. Breihan

YOUNGER BROTHERS

OUTLAWS OF THE OLD WEST

COMPLETE AND AUTHENTIC LIFE OF JESSE JAMES

THE DAY JESSE JAMES WAS KILLED

BADMEN OF THE FRONTIER DAYS

QUANTRILL AND HIS CIVIL WAR GUERRILLAS

Dedication

To Richard R. Riss II, dean of Western lore, authority on firearms of all ages, and possessor of the world's rarest and largest combined collection of authenticated outlaw and frontier guns, photographs, mementos and material ever assembled. His friendship and devotion to authenticity have made him a fellow traveler on old trails.

Publisher's Preface

GREAT GUNFIGHTERS OF THE WEST
was originally published in England and the British
phraseology and spelling have been retained to preserve the original flavor of the manuscript.

Contents

The Guns They Used

WILD BILL HICKOK
Early in life—.45-calibre Deane-Adams English 5-shot.
At McCanles' killing—Colt's 1851 Navy.
With Buffalo Bill—Two Colt's Frontier model, silver-plated, pearl-handled and engraved.
Personal, 1876—Pair of Remington 1875 Army and two Henry derringers.
Killed Phil Coe with a Williamson derringer, model 1866.
Wore when killed—Smith & Wesson Model No. 2, .32-calibre first issue, tip-up.
Buried with Sharps rifle, 1852 model.

WILD BILL LONGLEY
Dance .44-calibre 1863 model.
Colt's Frontier 1873 Army model.

CULLEN BAKER
Colt's 1848 model, .44-calibre 6-shot. Also carried at various times the Remington cap-and-ball percussion type revolver, and a percussion shotgun.

BAT MASTERSON
Colt's Frontier model 1873, 7½ in. barrel, silver-plated, pearl-handled and carved with Mexican eagle, marked 'W. B. Masterson'. Also .45-calibre Colt's Peacemaker.

HENRY STARR
Colt's Army .45 calibre (New Service model of 1909), walnut grip.

HENRY BROWN

Winchester 1873 model rifle, .44–.40 calibre. Sidearms usually were two Colt's single-action .45-calibre revolvers, 1873.

BEN THOMPSON

A handmade English shotgun. Also carried a single-action Colt's .45-calibre Frontier 1871 model (the Peacemaker), or the popular single-action Army 1873 .45 Colt's.

CLAY ALLISON

Colt's .45-calibre single-action Peacemaker. Also a heavy-slugged double-barrelled shotgun.

FRANK LESLIE

Colt's .45-calibre Peacemaker.

List of Illustrations

Between pages XII and 1

The Gunfighter: Prologue

THE GUNFIGHTER was a product of his time and his environment. He came from all parts of the United States—Hickok and Bat Masterson from Illinois; Allison from Tennessee; Longley from Texas; Henry Starr from Oklahoma Territory. Today many of them stand tall and invincible in the eyes of man and boy alike. But what spelled the difference between the fast gunslinger and his opponent? Was his name carved in the West's hall of fame because of his courage, speed, and accuracy or was it because there was a considerable degree of trickery and psychology in gunfighting?

We probably never will know who was the best gunfighter of the day. There were no electric timers and in many cases the winner was the one who started for his gun first. Quick reflexes depend upon good health, both mental and physical. No one is at his peak every day—as in the case of Wild Bill Hickok, who took to carrying a shotgun most of the time because his eyes had gone bad. A little-known fact is that he was totally blind for a time, due to a disease he had contracted and for which he was treated at the Army Hospital in Rochester, New York.

Many circumstances contributed to the coming of the gunfighter. Never content to remain rooted in one spot very long, the gunman was always looking over the next hill, always on the go, and, like water, he usually found his own level.

Everywhere the gunman was known, whether a lawman or an outlaw; his home was anywhere, along the cattle trails, in adobe dwellings, or in the dust-ridden towns of Wichita, Cimarron, Dodge City, Abilene, Caldwell, Hays City, and others of like reputation. Sometimes the gunslinger was a dashing poker-dealer or perhaps the man behind the badge. In remote areas, where civil law had not yet penetrated, the gunman was the law. His story is the real story of the West, not so much because he brought progress and wealth, but because he represented the form of person and life that the Americans in the East wanted to exist in the West. The timeless allure of the West caught the breath of the Easterners, those who craved to swagger down a boardwalk in high heels and to display their guns and Stetson hats. The West was romantic to those who knew little or nothing of it. The lurid hack writers of the day played up the scene and made it colourful.

The heyday of the gunfighter, regardless of what category he fitted into, lasted from the end of the Civil War until about 1900. Usually he was a young fellow, recently returned from war duty in the Union or Confederate Armies. Almost without exception he had learned the art of handling firearms even before he entered the war. When he returned he was an expert. He could draw his .45-calibre revolver from its holster, aim and fire it within split seconds. He had to know by instinct how to handle the six-gun and where to point it at the precise moment of squeezing the trigger. Without that exacting sense of direction he would soon be on Boot Hill.

Few scenes stir the imagination more than the picture of a dusty trail town street bordered by saloons, dens of vice, gambling casinos, with two intent men, hands poised over their holsters, advancing towards each other with deadly motives. The winner was the one who remained calm, took his time, and pulled the trigger just once. Such a shoot-out was not too common an affair, since a great many of the gunfights occurred in the saloons on the spur of the moment or sometimes even from ambush. An open gunfight was an exciting affair. Black powder was still in use, and often the gunfighter was enveloped in a weird cloud of dark smoke. Often if guns were fired at close range the powder-burns might ignite a man's clothing and there were times when the victim literally burned to death.

The professional gunfighter never notched his guns. He let willing others keep count for him, and sometimes that number was greatly increased as time passed. By virtue of his record the gunman was a marked man. Seldom the killing of an opponent settled any-thing—there were always others who wanted to try, be it a relative, friend, or merely a stranger who figured he was better than the top gun of the vicinity. The gunman had to watch every path for an ambush, note more details than the ordinary person would, and be cautious in his every move. He must sit with his back to the wall when playing poker. When Hickok failed to do this just once he was assassinated. Other great gunmen met the same fate because an ordinary gunfighter was afraid to tackle them—Billy the Kid Bonney, King Fisher, and Ben Thompson, for instance.

Some of the gunfighters possessed a blind courage. They were men born without knowing what fear meant, who thought they could master any living thing. Others were almost cowards. These depended upon a small reputation given them by their advantage over the ordinary man. Their kills represented the deaths of amateurs in the gunfighting game. Seldom, if ever, would they tackle a real professional. Many of them preferred an ambush, as did Billy the Kid when he killed Sheriff Brady at Lincoln, New Mexico.

A few of the noted gunmen had more than average intelligence, and usually possessed highly sensitive nervous systems. They faced the odds knowingly and willingly. Whether such a man was brave or simply driven on by will is a moot question. At any rate, he never was a normal individual. Only the best of them survived. Wyatt Earp, Bill Tilghman, and Bat Masterson lived to see the end of the gunfighters' era, and doubtlessly were happy to do so.

The Western novel and the movies have done much to distort the facts in regard to the gunmen of the old days, especially in the art of gun-fanning and firing two revolvers simultaneously. True, many of the gunmen carried two weapons and could shoot equally well with either hand. However, in a gunplay they would alternate their fire or empty one revolver and then use the other, sometimes reverting to the 'border shift' of throwing the loaded gun into their more efficient hand.

We know that Wild Bill Hickok carried weapons with the 'dogs' filed off, but there is little record of him being an expert fanner. Almost all students of the era believe that gun-fanning never existed or could exist, especially with single-action revolvers. Some of the old gunmen simply held their trigger tight against the guard, and then fanned the hammer with no lost motion. But to hit a small target using the fanning method is almost impossible. It impairs the accuracy of the weapon to fan it, even though it also makes a single-action weapon almost as fast as a double-action gun. In a shoot-out,

13

to fan a gun would be little short of murder. Pictorially, the fanner makes an exciting picture; in reality, it would be suicide. Most old-timer gunmen, outlaws, and lawmen seldom used the fanning method. They usually relied on the truth that one bullet would do all the damage needed if it was put in the right place.

The majority of the Western gunfighters chose to carry their pistols in holsters, but Hickok seldom or never used them. He carried two pistols in his waistband, their butts pointing inward for a cross-arm draw. Dallas Stoudenmire, the two-gun marshal of El Paso, carried his revolvers in special leather-lined hip-pockets. He could draw those lethal weapons with amazing speed. At one time he killed three men while under the deadly muzzle of a scattergun. He killed the shotgun man first and then got the other two. The noted Ben Thompson was prolific with any method of drawing. He used them all—holster, waistband, hip-pocket, and hideout gun. Legend has it that Ben was the inventor of the shoulder holster. Wes Hardin designed a vest with gun holsters in it. The vest was made of calfskin, with two holster pockets slanting outward from centre to hipbones, and holding two pistols, butts pointing inward. To draw, the arms were crossed and the guns plucked out.

Many of the Western gunmen, however, seem to have fallen into the category of psychological maniacs. Perhaps a knowledge of applied psychology might have helped them. Many embarked on careers of violence because they suffered inferiority complexes. Once the gunman started on his smoky road there was no turning back. That road led straight to Boot Hill, and normally a gunman's speed and clever gunplay merely postponed the trip. Once he killed, he had to kill again and again to retain his reputation and to save his own life. Others sought him out, hoping to boost their own standing by killing the man who killed so-and-so. Every man had his match. The question was: how long could he go before facing him?

It is morally wrong to make a hero of a killer. And yet frequently it is a thin hair that must be split in separating the killer from the professional gunfighter.

No killing can be justified; I am only trying to point out that in some cases it actually narrowed down to one thing—to kill or be killed.

The stories recorded herein are factual gatherings from musty old

14

records, yellowing newspapers, historical documents, personal interviews, and grassroot research. The final judgment is left to each individual. The reader must judge from his own inner sense of values and justice just how these men rated and where they stand in the annals of their time.

Top: Wild Bill Hickok. Only known photo in existence with signature. (Charles Rosamond Collection)

Bottom: Wild Bill Hickok's gun — .45 cal. Deane-Adams English 5-shot. (The Kansas State Historical Society, Topeka)

TOP: Wild Bill Longley

BOTTOM: Dance .44 cal. 1863 revolver used by Wild Bill Longley to kill his first man.

TOP: Bat Masterson in his later years. (Frontier Enterprises)

BOTTOM: Colt's 1848 model .44 cal. 6-shot similar to one used by Cullen Baker. (The Kansas State Historical Society, Topeka)

TOP: Henry Starr as a boy.

BOTTOM: 1909 Colt's Army .45 cal. used by Henry Starr in ill-fated attempt to rob People's National Bank, Arkansas, Feb. 18, 1921.

Top: Henry Brown as a marshal.

Bottom: Ben Wheeler's .44 SA Colt's revolver. (Harry Leah, Todmorden, Lancs., England)

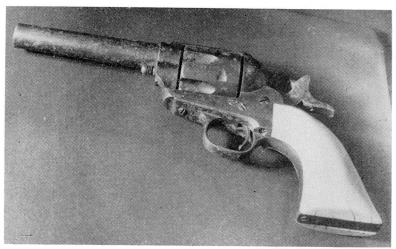

Top: Ben Thompson as marshal of Austin, Texas. (Frontier Enterprises)
Bottom: Ben Thompson's famous revolver. (K. D. Sacre, Atlanta, Ga.)

Top: Clay Allison from painting by Lon Pyrtle. (Frontier Enterprises)
Bottom: Clay Allison's Colt's .45 cal. revolver. (Terry Savage)

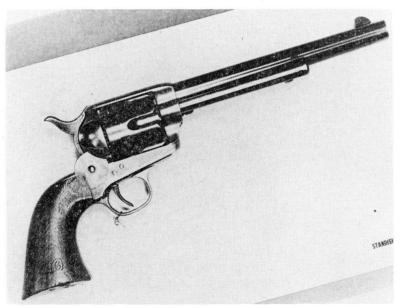

Top: Frank Leslie. (Frontier Enterprises)
Bottom: Frank Leslie's Colt's .45 cal. Peacemaker. (Frontier Enterprises)

TOP: Texas Street of Abilene in 1879.
CENTER: South Side Main St. of Ellsworth in 1867.
BOTTOM: Front Street of Dodge City in 1880's. (All photos: The Kansas State Historical Society)

Top: Building in San Antonio, Texas, where Ben Thompson was killed March 11, 1884.

Bottom: Birthplace of Wild Bill Hickok at Troy Grove, Ill.

Top: Trial of Jack McCall, the man who killed Wild Bill Hickok.
Bottom: Graves of Wild Bill Hickok, Calamity Jane and Potato Creek Johnny in Deadwood's Mt. Moriah "Boot Hill" Cemetery. (Black Hills Studios, Inc.)

Top: Ben Thompson's grave. (Frontier Enterprises)
Bottom Left: Henry Starr's grave and that of his child.
Bottom Right: Bat Masterson's grave.

.45-calibre Deane-Adams English 5-shot

1 Wild Bill Hickok

Dᴜʀɪɴɢ the year following the close of the American Civil War the name of a man flashed across the raw Western frontier like the descent of a shattered meteor. This man was Wild Bill Hickok, the enigma of the Border, who basked in the notoriety of his own imagination. The heat of this dubious fame was generated to gigantic proportions by the prolific pens of such contemporary thrill-writers as Ned Buntline, whose real name was Edward Zane Carol Judson, and Colonel George Ward Nicholas of Boston, Massachusetts.

Quick to sense the keen interest of the Eastern populace in the expanding West, such periodicals as *The Police Gazette* and *Harper's Weekly* climbed aboard the bandwagon and carried thrill-filled action stories of 'the world's greatest scout and gunfighter'. The tales were so fantastic and far-fetched that a number of hack writers must have been employed to grind them out. Hickok wanted to be fair with his public, and tried to some degree to live up to the reputation tailor-made for him. So the legends grew and grew until only the Greek myths could match them. Yet the true story of Bill has another hue, one that is not all glossy and bright.

William Alonzo Hickok—according to the family Bible, the name was spelled Haycock—Bill's father, was a deacon in the Presbyterian Church and was born December 5, 1801, at North Hero, Grand Isle County, Vermont, and passed away in 1852. He married Polly Butler in 1827 and they had six children, four sons and two daughters.

James Butler Hickok, later to become the fabulous Wild Bill, was born on May 27, 1837, in Iowa,[1] La Salle County, Illinois, where he remained on a farm until 1855. From his boyhood days Bill disclosed a marked fondness for firearms; when fourteen years old he secured an excellent pistol, and a short time later his father presented him with a first-class rifle. Very few books were obtainable in that part of the country. *The Life of Kit Carson* and *The Trapper's Guide* made such an impression on James Hickok's mind that he told his friends: 'One day I'll beat anything that Kit Carson ever did or attempted!'

From that day on Hickok lived a life filled with violence and strife until his death in 1876. He became accustomed to the rough life of the frontier, and in 1855 joined General James Lane of the Free Staters. At that time the Kansas Jayhawkers rode into Missouri to plunder and to steal. Another segment of the border ruffians was a division called the Red Legs because they wore bright red leggings to identify themselves. Later during the Civil War these factions clashed with the notorious William Clarke Quantrill of the Missouri Raiders. Young Hickok joined the Red Legs and assumed the first name of his father, William. There has been much discussion as to why Hickok was called Wild Bill when his name was James. However, this sobriquet was acquired while he was using his father's name.

Many writers have claimed his famous nickname stemmed from his bravery and daring at the Rock Creek Station affair, but such is not the case. During a riot while in Leavenworth, Kansas, Bill was instrumental in disposing of several men. But where others were content to vanquish an opponent, Bill was not satisfied unless he maimed the man. During this affair an excited woman spectator yelled: 'Give him hell, Wild Bill!' So his new name was born amid violence and death.

After his association with the Kansas Red Legs Bill became constable of Monticello Township, Johnson County, where he had taken up a claim and tried his hand at farming. It was during the official term of his first job as a peace officer that he told Mrs. George Armstrong Custer he had slain six men during the Leavenworth fracas—his first killings. Already young Bill had acquired a vivid imagination; it was to grow.

[1] Now Troy Grove, Illinois.

18

Tiring of an uneventful existence, Hickok hired out as a wagon-driver on the Santa Fe Trail. He drove stages over the Overland Trail and had many an occasion to use his weapons. There is little on record concerning this portion of his life. In the autumn of 1860 he was mauled by a grizzly bear in Raton Pass. Bill's employers, Russell, Majors, and Waddell, had the young man taken to Santa Fe and later returned to Kansas City, where he slowly began to recover from the injuries.

Early in March of 1861, then twenty-three, Hickok arrived at Rock Creek, on the Overland route, where he had been sent by his employers to do lighter work on account of his injuries. David Colbert McCanles was then in charge, and assigned Bill to work as a helper at the stables.

For some unknown reason McCanles disliked Hickok from the first. He took every occasion to humiliate the young man. He gave him various nicknames, one of which was 'Duck Bill', due to Hickok's protruding upper lip. He would also seize Bill when there were crowds of men present, wrestle with him, and then throw him down. Bill could not do much about it, for his left arm was still disabled, and it was only with pain that he moved about at all. McCanles pretended that this was all in fun, but there was malice behind his every movement. He continued this course to within a few days of his death. Others claimed that Hickok was lazy and neglected the stock and that he and McCanles got into many arguments because of it.

Hickok's temper was far from even. He could not bear to be called Duck Bill. This fact has significance because little credit has hitherto been given to Jack McCall's story that he killed Hickok to avenge the death of his brother.

Near Rock Creek lived the widow McCall and her two small sons, Jack, twelve, and Andy, nine. One day young Andy called to Hickok: 'Howdy, Mr. Duck Bill.'

Hickok flew into a rage and ran after the lad, striking him on the head with a hoe. The blow proved fatal.

'I'll kill you when I grow up!' cried Jack McCall. We all know how he lived up to this threat.

Nebraska Territory in 1861 had no real law, so Hickok was never brought to justice for his crime. Mrs. McCall made frantic efforts

19

to have something done about Andy's killing, but with the whole country in heated discussion over the slavery question and civil war, not much attention was paid to her pleas.

On May 1, 1861, McCanles sold his place to Russell, Majors, and Waddell, who appointed Horace Wellman superintendent. Hickok and one Doc Brink were engaged as hostlers. McCanles moved to his ranch on the Little Blue, at the mouth of Rock Creek.

McCanles had a mistress living in a cabin at the West Rock Creek Ranch, across from where Hickok was employed. He had become aware of the relations between McCanles and Miss Sarah Shull—Kate Shell—soon after his arrival at Rock Creek, and he kept informed as to the exact nature of the relationship. Taking advantage of what he knew, he made progress for himself in the good graces of the pretty woman. McCanles became suspicious of Hickok and in his furious jealousy devised a means to discover the truth. Afterwards he regarded Hickok with a deadly hatred.

When McCanles moved to the ranch on the Little Blue, Miss Shull lived for a month or two at the West Rock Creek Station, where she was visited by Hickok. McCanles had knowledge of his visits at once, and he promptly warned Hickok to keep away from Miss Shull, and not to cross the creek to the West Ranch under pain of death. Bill confessed to two of his intimate friends that there was no room in his heart for any woman other than Sarah Shull. He was always looking for her, hoping to see her, take her in his arms, have her for his own. It is probable that, after she left Rock Creek, Sarah never gave Bill another thought. It was something he came to realize later, but it never changed him.

It was on the afternoon of July 12, 1861, that McCanles told Sarah Shull he was going to 'clean up' on the people at the station. It is not known exactly what he meant by the expression. The stage company still owed McCanles money for the Rock Creek Station. Perhaps he meant he was going to get his money, perhaps that he meant to fight them. Yet the latter explanation would not square with the record that the McCanles party was unarmed during the subsequent affray. McCanles was accompanied by his cousin, James Woods, and by James Gordon, an employee. He also took along his young son, Monroe, which bolsters the belief that the men were not armed. Certainly McCanles would not endanger the life of his own boy.

Apologists for Hickok claim the party was armed and that McCanles approached the station in a belligerent manner and demanded his money. Legally he had a right to evict the people there and to reclaim his property. The stage company had defaulted in its payment of the agreed sum at a stipulated time.

At the station the McCanles group met only the common-law Mrs. Wellman. She stated her husband was absent, that he had not returned from Jacksonville, where he had gone in an effort to get the money due McCanles. The visitor could tell she lied. At this point Hickok appeared on the scene. He pushed Mrs. Wellman aside and confronted McCanles. His appearance surprised the enraged man, and must have had a sobering effect upon him, for he stopped to parley. The fact that McCanles believed Hickok elsewhere that day adds more credibility to the report that he was not armed. McCanles bore no killing hatred against the others at Rock Creek Station. He had threatened only Hickok.

'What in hell have you got to do with this?' he snapped.

'The station's business is my business,' replied Bill, 'and I don't intend to see you bully Wellman or his wife.'

'My business is with Wellman, not you, and if you want to take a hand in it come on out here, and we'll settle it like men.'

McCanles knew that Wellman was in the house, that Mrs. Wellman's story was but a stall, and he was uneasy. Perhaps a weapon was aimed at him, covering his every move.

'Send Wellman out here so I can settle with him, or I'll come in and drag him out!' he shouted.

There was danger, he knew now, so he walked from the west door to the south or front door. From there he had a view of the interior of the whole house, except that portion shut off by the calico curtain. In the west room, the kitchen, was Sarah Shull—who later said she was two miles away at the time—and Sarah Kelsey, a stepdaughter of one Joe Baker, who had been employed by McCanles.

McCanles stepped into the south doorway, from which position Wellman and Hickok were in sight. He did not attack them, and he could think of nothing better to justify his presence than to ask for a drink of water—which clearly was an excuse, for there was a bucket of water with a dipper in it two feet away. Hickok left Wellman, went to the bucket, dipped up a gourdful of water, and handed it to McCanles. Then he turned and walked stealthily back towards the curtain. McCanles had not really wanted water. He dropped the dipper and called upon Hickok to wait. Hickok ignored the request. He was soon behind the curtain, where he had every advantage. McCanles realized the danger in which he stood. Now Hickok called back to McCanles that if he came in to drag him out: 'There will be one less son-of-a-bitch when you try that!'

It will never be known whether McCanles started in to drag Hickok out, for almost immediately a shot was fired from behind the curtain, and the bullet went through McCanles' chest. He staggered and fell backwards in the yard. Notwithstanding his mortal wound, McCanles attempted to raise himself up, and was helped by his son Monroe, who had run to his aid.

'Run, son, run! Your life's in danger here. I'm a goner! Hurry— get going now!' McCanles commanded the boy.

With that, young Monroe took off at a good sprint and disappeared in a nearby gully. Probably it was fortunate that he obeyed promptly, for he might have fallen another victim to Bill's blood-lust.

When Gordon and Woods heard the shot and saw McCanles fall they left the barn and ran at full speed to the house. Woods attempted to enter by the kitchen door, which was the west door, where McCanles had first appeared. Gordon ran to the south door. Woods was mortally wounded when Hickok shot him twice with his revolver. Gordon came up just in time to see Hickok shoot Woods. He tried to make a run for it. Hickok fired and Gordon fell to the ground. One of the others picked up a grubbing hoe and quickly extinguished any life that was left in the wounded Gordon.

Often it was said afterwards that James Butler Hickok killed nine of the McCanles gang of horse thieves who attacked the Rock Creek Station to steal horses for the Confederacy. That is not true. The whole affair was really McCanles *versus* Hickok, a showdown between the two. Both were men of destiny, strong, fitted to stand in the forefront of the frontier's advance—to take the lead of civilization into new lands. By his later courage, his intrepidity, his iron will, his marvellous personal achievement, Wild Bill won fame. By his strength of character and his tragic death, McCanles won fame. One was a knight of the Middle Ages, strangely out of time; the other a freebooter with the daring to take what he wanted regardless of the consequences. Both will live on in the pages of the West's history.

Many have questioned the record which clearly depicts Hickok as a sadistic killer at the time of the Rock Creek affair. The official files are still intact in Nebraska, but were not located until many years after Bill was raised on his pedestal of fame. The still-existing records show that a complaint was filed, and was the first heard in Gage County, Nebraska Territory. It reads as follows:

> *Territory of Nebraska*
> *County of Gage S.S.*
> The complainant and informant, LeRoy McCanles, of the county of Johnson, Territory aforesaid, made before T. M. Coulter, Esquire, one of the Justices of the Peace, in and for Gage County, on the 13th day of July, 1861, who being duly sworn on his oath says . . . That the crime of murder has been committed in the county of Jones, and that Dutch Bill . . . Doc . . . and Wellman (their other names unknown) Committed the same. . . .
>
> J. L. MCCANLES
> Subscribed and sworn to before me this 13th day of July 1861.
>
> T. M. COULTER,
> Justice of the Peace.

Upon this complaint Justice of the Peace Coulter then made out an order of arrest, which was served, and a record made and duly filed:

> The warrant . . . the within warrant . . . came to hand this 13th day of July, 1861, at 2.00 o'clock p.m.
> Served the within warrant by arresting the within Dutch Bill, Doc, and Wellman this 15th day of July, 1861.
>
> E. B. HENDEE,
> Sheriff of Gage County
> Nebraska Territory
> Sheriff's fee $5.00

Hickok (Dutch or Duck Bill), Doc Brink, and Horace Wellman were placed in custody on July 15, 1861, at Rock Creek Ranch, which

23

lay six miles south-east of the present city of Fairbury, Nebraska. They were loaded into a wagon and driven to Beatrice, and on July 18 their case was given a preliminary hearing, of which record still exists. Brink and Wellman were accused as accessaries to the crime of murder. It might be mentioned that most chroniclers of Hickok's career have declared that Wild Bill never was arrested for a crime. This rather sets the record straight.

The prisoners were held over for the Circuit Court, but the trial never took place. The start of the Civil War and the quick departure of Miss Shull from the territory provided interruptions. All the same, the fantasy constructed from Wild Bill's performance as a gunfighter at Rock Creek is now seen for what it was. The famous fight was in truth a massacre. Hickok's stature is somewhat lessened. He decamped and left for St. Louis, Missouri, and never returned to the vicinity of Rock Creek, except once when scouting for the Union army.

In August 1861 Hickok became a brigade wagon-master under the command of General John C. Fremont, in command at Fort Leavenworth. He seemed to take his work seriously and General Custer had this to say of Wild Bill:

Whether on foot or on horseback, he was one of the most perfect types of physical manhood I ever saw. Of his courage there could be no question. His skill in the use of the rifle and pistol was unerring. His deportment was entirely free from all bluster or bravado. He never spoke of himself unless requested to do so. His conversation never bordered upon the vulgar or blasphemous.

His influence among the frontiersmen was unbounded; his word was law; and many are the personal quarrels and disturbances which he has checked among his comrades by the simple announcement that 'this has gone far enough', if need be, followed by the ominous warning that, if persisted in, the quarreller 'must settle with me'.

Wild Bill always carried two handsome, ivory-handled revolvers of the large size. He was never seen without them. I have a personal knowledge of at least a half a dozen men whom he has at various times killed, others have been seriously wounded—yet he always escaped unhurt in every encounter.

Custer being as great a showman as Hickok himself, this sounds like something the General would say.

Wild Bill Hickok

Amazing yarns have been told of Hickok's service as a Union scout and spy. The most famous include how he dashed through large bodies of Confederate soldiers or Quantrill guerillas, laid half of them low, then managed to escape without a scratch; or how he crawled into the enemy camp, obtained information of the utmost secrecy, and returned unharmed to help win a major battle. It does not stand to reason that all that has been written about him could have happened. The odds against one man performing so spectacularly are too great. Regardless of one man's amazing proficiency or uncanny ability to handle weapons, he could not have escaped all the bullets supposedly fired at Hickok during his Civil War escapades. Probably the most incredible of Bill's Civil War exploits was his sharpshooting at the Battle of Pea Ridge, Arkansas, March 6–8, 1862. The Union forces under General Curtis were battling with the Confederates under Generals Sterling Price and Benjamin McCulloch.

Hickok's commanding officer instructed him to find an advantageous spot overlooking Cross Timber Hollow and to pick off as many of the enemy as he could. Crawling to the protection of some heavy timber, Hickok began to fire at the Confederates. For several hours he picked off grey-clad soldiers until he had downed a total of thirty-six. By that time it seems the enemy felt they had a formidable sharpshooter taking heavy toll. General McCulloch ordered a charge against the hidden Union rifleman. But before the charge could become effective Hickok shot and killed McCulloch, demoralized his men, and was able to escape.

There can be no question that Hickok risked his life daily for the Union cause, as did many thousands of other faithful men. Of course, Hickok was singled out to become the champion because of his glib talk, his expert way of making a mountain out of a mole-hill, and his growing reputation as a fighter. Bill had no scruples worth mentioning. One day while he was riding through a small Missouri town an old man poked his head from an upstairs window and yelled: 'Hurrah for Jeff Davis!' Hickok took a single shot at the man and killed him.

A search of the Federal War Records indicates that Hickok was a satisfactory scout for General Curtis, but nothing is recorded of his amazing escapes or his ability to outwit the enemy at every turn.

Discharged from the service in 1864, Hickok returned to Spring-field, Missouri, but the welcome mat was not laid out as he had expected. In the history of Greene County we find that Hickok was unpopular with the citizens. There is one account which gives this picture of him:

Duck Bill provoked trouble wherever he could. He had a room at the Lyons' house, where he delighted in terrorizing the guests by his bullying and swaggering ways. He was by nature a ruffian, soon to become a drunken, swaggering fellow who delighted, when on a spree, in frightening nervous men and timid women by riding on horseback on the sidewalks and into the saloons, hotels, and other public places.

The *Kansas City Star* carried the following uncomplimentary piece about Hickok:

On one occasion a 300-pound foreigner, named Phillador, who operated a saloon on South Street in Springfield, rushed from behind the bar just as Hickok came riding through the swinging door of his place, grabbed the horse's bridle and backed him on to the sidewalk. Bill dis-mounted and came into the saloon, calling vile names at the saloon-keeper, who drew a knife with one hand and slapped Bill's face with the other. Turning his back on Bill, he said, 'Shoot me in the back, that is your way, but I'll kill you before I die.'

It was in Springfield that Hickok had his fight with an Arkansas man named Dave Tutt. Bill had been friendly with Dave's pretty sister, but when an old acquaintance of Bill's arrived in town he discarded Tutt's sister and made plans to romance the new arrival, Susanna Moore.

Susanna was friendly with Hickok, but suddenly the relationship was broken off and she became more interested in Tutt. This infuriated Hickok, who needed only an excuse to kill someone. Tutt knew this, but did not fear Bill's supposed reputation as a scout and gunslinger. On July 21, 1865, the two men clashed in the town's square. Rumour mentioned a supposed gambling quarrel, but the main reason was Susanna Moore.

Hickok and Tutt were seventy-five yards from each other when Tutt fired at Hickok and missed. Calmly Hickok rested his gunhand upon his left arm to steady it and shot Dave through the heart. This range immediately placed Hickok in the category of a cool and deadly marksman. These were not the quick-draw tactics for which Hickok has gone down in tradition. The authorities decided the slaying was justifiable, and Hickok went free.

A week later Colonel Nicholas arrived in Springfield, eager to find an exciting gunman or outlaw to provide a feature for *Harper's*. So far he had been unsuccessful. No deadly gunman infested the West, it was too early. They were yet to come. Something had to be concocted. The people in the East were accustomed to reading bloody accounts of the Civil War, and they wanted more in the same vein, regardless of how it was served up. Nicholas decided that if he could not find the right man he would create one. His opportunity came quicker than he had anticipated. One day when seated outside his hotel he noticed a tall, handsome man astride a fine mount. He later said the figure appeared more like that of a woman than of a man. His curiosity was genuinely aroused.

A former Union officer stationed at Springfield, Nicholas had no trouble in finding out about Hickok. The hotel proprietor told him of the Tutt killing.

'Excellent!' cried the colonel. 'Just what I need. See that we're introduced.'

It was during the interview that was arranged that Hickok told the fantastic tale of wiping out, single-handed, the terrible McCanles gang of horse thieves at Rock Creek Station. The lurid and grossly misleading account was later published in *Harper's Weekly*.[1] Colonel Nicholas introduced the article by saying: 'I have checked carefully into the account and have interviewed eyewitnesses . . . I am convinced this entire story is true.'

What the colonel failed to mention was that in less than five hours after the Rock Creek affair S. J. Alexander, Secretary of State, and D. C. Jenkins, Member of the State Legislature, arrived there to investigate the affair. Instead of ten dead ruffians, as told by Hickok, they found three murdered men.

Overnight, Hickok was skyrocketed to fame. The great *New York Herald* sent Henry Stanley to interview the 'hero of the plains'. Rival newspapers and periodicals so twisted and warped the facts concerning Wild Bill Hickok that it is now impossible to tell where

[1] Vol. 34, February 1867.

truth ended and fiction began. Bill took full advantage of his popularity. He discarded his buckskins and took to wearing corsets, Prince Albert coat, checkered trousers, silk waistband, and a flower-lined cape. Again leaning to his feminine inclinations, Bill sported high-heeled shoes and wore his blond hair long and flowing.

One of Wild Bill's most ardent admirers was Mrs. Custer, wife of General Custer. It was chiefly through her intercession that Hickok was appointed a deputy United States marshal operating out of Fort Riley, Kansas. His job was to work against the horse thieves infesting that area. The official records show that he did a good job of bringing in rustlers and Army deserters, sometimes battling it out with them.

During the years of 1867-8 Hickok was a scout for General Hancock in his campaign against the Indians. As a Government courier he risked his life daily in his secret treks through Indian country to obtain information for his commanding officer. Had the hack writers of the day stuck to facts about Hickok no doubt many interesting and true stories could have been written, possibly more absorbing than those dished out in fable form. Now no one knows what to believe, or even whether to believe any of the accepted legend. There seems to be no accurate account of Hickok's experiences during those two years, so most of the legend writers have based their incredible stories about him on events supposed to have happened in that short period.

Like a rolling snowball, the legends grew and grew. Soon Hickok began to tire of running messages for the Government and decided to bask in his fame. Everywhere he went the newspapermen followed and interviewed him. In the gambling houses of Topeka, Kansas City, and Leavenworth the crowds gaped in amazement at this Eighth Wonder of the world. Men who hardly knew his name suddenly had known him all their life; those who knew him slightly had been his neighbours at one time or another.

In May 1869 Wild Bill swaggered into Hays City, Kansas, a rough-and-tumble town badly in need of law and order, civic virtues it had not acquired. The local politicians prevailed upon Hickok to place his name on the ballot for sheriff. In August he was elected sheriff, with headquarters at Hays City. He was also automatically appointed the town marshal. Bill displayed skill and cunning in his policing of Hays City, but there is no factual record giving any account of fast-draw shoot-outs and such exploits as the movies and contemporary writers would have us believe. Like the gunmen who followed him, Hickok devised all sorts of tricks to throw an adversary off balance or distract him for a fleeting second. He tried to seek out the little, unnoticed failings of his foe, thereby usually having the slight edge on his opponent.

The most talked about killing by Hickok while in Hays City was the shooting of an all-around badman named Jack Strawhan. No details have been found concerning the animosity between the two, but it appears to have stemmed from some altercation they had in Ellsworth, Kansas. Strawhan did not fear Hickok's reputation and swore to kill him on sight. He entered a saloon, looking for Wild Bill. Hickok saw his enemy, but made no motion to draw. Strawhan, thinking he had not been observed, pulled a pistol. Before he could fire Hickok drew his revolver and killed him. Some reports claim that Hickok shot Strawhan before the latter had drawn. The news spread quickly. 'Hickok had drawn with lightning speed and slain his adversary in a matter of seconds.' Hickok was soon resting on his laurels. His reputation had preceded him to every place he stayed, and men who dared to face him did so nervously, the 'Hickok reputation' weighing heavily upon them. This was a decided advantage to Wild Bill.

Hickok's career in Hays City came to an abrupt end when he tangled with General Custer's brother, an officer in the Seventh Cavalry, who felt that his Army authority rendered him immune to civil authority. He rode drunkenly up and down the streets of the town, shooting at will. Hickok took the officer into custody, something that appeared outrageous to Custer, and he felt humiliated. With five of his soldier friends Custer descended upon the saloon. One of the soldiers lunged at Hickok, while others caught him from behind. Wild Bill was able to draw his pistol, and he killed one of the men behind him. His second shot killed the soldier to his right, and before some of the townspeople could interfere he had slain another of the soldiers.

General Sheridan ordered Hickok to be arrested, dead or alive. But the wily Wild Bill had taken leave of Hays City some minutes after the fracas. He hid out for a while near Ellsworth.

Spring of 1871 found Hickok at Abilene, Kansas, where he secured a room at the Alamo Hotel and became a regular customer at the gaming tables. Abilene had been without a satisfactory marshal since the death of the famed Tom Smith, the man who tamed the town with his bare fists. Smith had been waylaid and killed by two ruffians named Joe Hammer and Mac McConnell on November 2, 1870. News that Hickok was living at the Alamo reached the anxious ears of Mayor Joseph McCoy, whose duty it was to appoint a new marshal. Former Mayor T. C. Henry did not approve of Hickok, saying that Tom Smith was genuine and believed in law and order, while Hickok was a poseur and a killer.

Mayor McCoy noticed how the crowds gathered before the Alamo, anxious to get a look at the famous Wild Bill Hickok. And truly he was something to look at. He was as perfect a specimen of manhood as ever walked, and often dressed as a regular frontier dude. His six feet two inches were perfectly proportioned. He was wide-shouldered, lean of waist, with hands and feet as small as a woman's. His blond hair hung over his shoulders, and his blue-grey eyes pierced through one. McCoy was more interested in Hickok's reputation and his guns. He finally was able to persuade the City Council to back him in offering Wild Bill a hundred and fifty dollars a month for his services as Marshal of Abilene, Kansas. Hickok accepted the job, and a more sinister and deadly atmosphere of law enforcement very soon hung over the town. The date of his appointment was April 15, 1871. It was to be an exciting year for Wild Bill Hickok.

Abilene, Kansas, in July 1871 was as tough as a Western town could get. Since most cowtrails led to and ended at Abilene, it was there that the cowpokes blew off steam they had built up over the long, dry months on the cattle-drives. There, too, was the notorious Bull's Head Saloon, owned by Ben Thompson and Phil Coe.

Along with the herds of Johnson and Carol came the notorious gunslinger John Wesley Hardin. At Abilene Hardin was requested by his employers to remain on to round up the strays. He agreed and was also quick in establishing his reputation in the town. The first night he and his boss went out Carol got into an argument with a police officer named Carson, who pulled his gun and ordered Carol to jail. Wes Hardin quickly covered him and promptly told him if he

30

was looking for trouble to go get Hickok and come back. The officer left, but didn't return.

Thompson, a deadly enemy of Hickok, saw a situation which he might turn into a profitable shooting match. He told young Hardin that Hickok was passing the word around that he intended to shoot Wes in the back at the first chance offered. Hardin, however, refused to be goaded into a shooting match with Hickok on Thompson's unsupported word. He didn't seek out Hickok, but he didn't side-step him, either. Despite a Hickok ordinance that guns were not permitted in the town limits, Wes Hardin wore his pistols every-where he went. The saloon-keepers complained to Hickok, and the marshal finally stopped Hardin as he was leaving a saloon one morning and ordered him to hand over his guns. Hardin calmly pulled his pistols out and handed them towards Hickok, butts first. As the marshal reached for them, Hardin suddenly twirled the guns on his fingers, and Hickok was staring into the barrels. Wild Bill and the townspeople gathered around were frozen by Hardin's deftness. It was one time when Hickok had to back down. He slowly returned his guns to their holsters. A number of the people in the crowd yelled at Wes Hardin to shoot Hickok down, for he was not popular with some elements in Abilene. Wes ignored the crowd and told Hickok he had heard the marshal was planning on gunning him in the back when the chance presented itself. Hickok denied the accusation, and the two men finally stepped into a private room in one of the saloons to talk things over. They parted friends, and a few minutes later Wes was in another saloon drinking. Later on an attempt was made to murder Hardin as he slept in his hotel room. Before dawn on July 7 Hardin heard someone unlock his door and creep into the room. Light was reflected from the blade of a dagger in the hand of his would-be assassin. Hardin always slept light and with a gun under his pillow. As his assailant approached the bed Hardin rolled to the floor and emptied his pistol into him. Wes Hardin never knew for certain who his assailant was, but years later in Huntsville Prison he wrote a letter in which he accused Wild Bill Hickok of hiring the assassin.

Bill had the run of pretty women in Abilene, and the cause of his next trouble was another woman. His old flame Susanna Moore, from Springfield, had come to Abilene to share a cottage with him.

She bore no grudge for his killing of Dave Tutt. Also there was Mrs. Agnes Lake, who brought a theatrical company to the trail herd town, and she fell hard for Hickok. An attractive woman named Jessie Hazel, operator of an expensive bawdy house, caused Phil Coe and Hickok to fall out. Others claimed that accusations of bribery and fixed gambling wheels in the Bull's Head Saloon brought about the rivalry. Things came to a head when Jessie Hazel moved her belongings into the expensive hotel rooms where Thompson and Coe lived. On October 5 Phil Coe announced that he was leaving for Texas and taking Jessie with him. This was another bitter pill for the proud and sensitive Hickok to swallow.

In the evening of that same day the jovial Texans were having a merry time celebrating their departure and Phil Coe having found himself a loving woman. All this rankled with Wild Bill, who would have no part of the festivities. They found him at the Alamo Hotel, but he refused to go with them. After leaving Wild Bill the crowd went west on First Street to Cedar. A noisy dog got mixed up in the crowd and bit Coe in the ankle. The enraged Texan shot and killed the animal.

At the sound of the shot Wild Bill came charging from the hotel, wanting to know who had fired a gun.

Coe still had his weapon in his hand, and informed Bill that he had just killed a dog. Perhaps the sight of the pistol in Coe's hand unnerved Hickok. At any rate, he grabbed his pistols and the fight was on. The two men emptied their guns at each other. One bullet went between Hickok's legs and another over his head, knocking his hat off. One man in the crowd was killed and two were wounded. Hickok's last bullet hit Coe in the groin. He died of blood poisoning two days later. Had Coe been sober, no doubt Bill's career would have ended then and there. It was on this occasion that Bill also killed his trusted friend, Mike Williams, who came running to assist him. Hickok thought he was someone else, fired, and killed him.

This fight was the peak of Hickok's career as a gunman. Most people said he lost his nerve completely afterwards. He took to carrying a sawed-off shotgun, a regular shotgun, and two pistols, as well as a Bowie knife in his waistband.

On December 13 the City Council of Abilene discharged Wild

Bill Hickok as marshal, stating they had no further need of his services. To sum up Hickok's activities in Abilene we have the following report by Stuart Henry, brother of T. G. Henry, Abilene's first mayor:

Wild Bill's headquarters were in the palatial Alamo Saloon, only a block from our house. He gambled there as one visible means of support. The town trustees appointed him marshal since no one else came forth . . . the choice did not prove satisfactory to the citizens, still mourning the death of Tom Smith. Grave misgivings did they feel, for Hickok consorted entirely with criminals or the law-breakers, cheek by jowl with Texans and 'badmen'. He lived outside the civic life. The Abilene citizens regarded him as a desperado and argued whether 'Texas Jack' surpassed him as a badman.

Smith's effective regime of disarmament the summer before, his almost perfect control, made Hickok's line of duty far easier than Smith's . . . but since his interests and time were divided by gambling, he did not remain strict about the gun-carrying ordinance . . . residents gradually got accustomed again to the pistol-toting and the shots at night.

Wild Bill did not patrol Texas Street either on horseback or on foot. He stayed in the Alamo at his games . . . the proprietor of the theatre next door felt so uncertain of Bill's handling the town efficiently that he went to the expense of employing an officer for his own place. If wanted, Wild Bill had to be looked up in the Alamo Saloon. He was not a trained police officer . . . he did not fancy taking a culprit or offender to the Justice of the Peace to deal with. He acted only too ready to shoot down, to kill outright —conceptions of courts, the right of trial by jury, appeared to lie beyond his conscience or experience . . . he did not see why as marshal he could not sit in public poker games . . . so Texas Street simmered. . . .

In 1874 Hickok drifted east at the invitation of Ned Buntline and joined Ned's show, *Scouts of the Prairie*, as did Buffalo Bill Cody. However, Bill's eyes were going bad on him and he was nearly blind. Cody had always been a lukewarm friend of Hickok, but when Wild Bill actually needed help Cody threw him out. Wild Bill said: 'I wish I had killed that son-of-a-bitch when I had the chance years ago.'

Many persons have expressed disbelief concerning the fact that Hickok was going blind from a disease. Yet the records show that he went to the medical authorities at Camp Carlin, Wyoming, to have

C   33

his eyes treated. The report was: 'Advanced glaucoma in left eye and soon would be completely blind.'

After leaving the Buntline show Hickok returned to Wyoming and took up residence in Laramie County. It was in this state that his first real love affair bloomed, amid a display of bravery and violence. During a performance of a lion show conducted by the then-famous Lake Troupe, Bill leaped into the ring to rescue from the jaws of a maddened African lion Mrs. Agnes Lake Thatcher, who had known him in Abilene. Three well-placed slugs from his Colt .45 disposed of the king of beasts permanently. This incident must have caused Bill to realize something else, for on March 2, 1876, he said to the owner of the McDaniel's Variety Theatre in Cheyenne: 'My shooting days are over. The best I can do now is to see a man's form indistinctly at sixteen paces.'

On March 5 Hickok married Agnes Lake Thatcher. She gave her age as forty-two, her residence as Cincinnati, Ohio. Bill gave his age as forty-five, raising it with his usual chivalry, his residence as Laramie County, Wyoming. They were united in marriage by Rev. W. F. Warren, of the Methodist Episcopal Church.

Needing finances, Hickok agreed to guide a group of one hundred would-be miners from Cheyenne to the Black Hills. Worrying about his eyes he tried some target practice along the route of the stages he was guiding. His aim was fairly good and his actions were amusing the passengers. Bill had only two cartridges left in each of his revolvers when the group was set upon by a band of five outlaws, led by Frank Culley, an old enemy.

One by one, Bill disposed of four of the bandits. Then his guns clicked empty. Culley, close enough to hear the click of the guns, grinned gleefully in anticipation of shooting the great Wild Bill Hickok. Culley's eyes left Wild Bill for only an instant, but that was the break Hickok needed. With all his strength Bill hurled one of his empty revolvers at the outlaw, hitting him on the head and crushing his skull.

Later Hickok laughed as he brought to mind the words of Buckshot Roberts, the expert rifleman of New Mexico, who was killed by Billy the Kid's henchmen: 'The only thing a six-shooter is good for is to throw at someone.'

Hickok's marriage to Mrs. Thatcher did not last very long. Some records indicate that Wild Bill had no real yearning for women; that their passionate demands annoyed him. Also, he thought Mrs. Thatcher was rich. Later he told his men friends that Mrs. Thatcher was too old to have any sex passion left.

Hickok naturally was a gambler, so he and Colorado Charlie Utter left for Deadwood, South Dakota, to get in on the ground floor of the new gold strike. Utter could shoot rings around Hickok. Charlie could hit a dime a hundred feet away, nine times out of ten. Once, while riding on horseback through Hays City, he fired six shots from his pistol at a knothole in a telegraph pole, and all six bullets struck the knothole. Few men have ever matched Charlie for marksmanship. On the other hand, Wyatt Earp claimed to have seen Hickok place six bullets in the letter 'O' of a sign hanging about a hundred yards away. He said Hickok held his gun as almost every man skilled in such matters preferred to hold one when in action: with a half-bent elbow that brought the gun slightly in front of his body at about, or slightly above, the level of the waist.

In Deadwood, in addition to being a gambler, Bill's reputation allowed him and his self-styled peace officers to enforce what they called law and order.

On August 1 Hickok sat down in a draw-poker game with a man known as 'Buffalo Curly', not recognizing him as the Jack McCall of Rock Creek Station! Ordinarily, McCall wouldn't have had enough money to take part in the average game of poker that went on almost continuously in Saloon No. 66, owned by Carl Mann and Jerry Lewis. But on this particular occasion the game was for small stakes. Bill played more to pass away the time than with a thought of winning much.

Some claim that Wild Bill won five hundred dollars from McCall, but that does not seem to compare with Jack's reputation of always being broke. At the time he killed Hickok, McCall was a typical saloon bum and 'moocher' of free drinks and lunches, living a more or less hand-to-mouth existence. He worked as a part-time saloon swamper, and his duties in the Lewis and Mann Saloon consisted of sweeping the floor, mopping it, and doing the menial work that is necessary in such an establishment.

On Wednesday, August 2, another game of draw poker was in session at Saloon No. 66, a four-handed game. This game was

35

destined to be long remembered by those who seek the favours of the goddess of chance. It produced the draw-poker hand that was to become famous as 'The Dead Man's Hand'.

In that game, besides Hickok, there were Charley Rich, Carl Mann, and Captain Massey, the latter a Missouri steamboat pilot. When he entered the saloon Hickok stopped to chat with bartender Harry Young, and being the last to seat himself at the card table he had to take a seat with his back to the door. So unusual was this position to Bill, who always sat with his back to a wall, that he requested Charley Rich to change places with him. Charley jokingly accused Bill of being superstitious, and good-naturedly declined to exchange places.

A little after three in the afternoon Jack McCall entered. His manner was care-free, and he gave no indication of his murderous intention, but with calculating care he walked up to the bar and then cut to the table where the four players were seated. With an anxious glance around, to see that no one was watching, he took a position directly behind the chair occupied by Wild Bill.

McCall had been standing behind the chair for only a short while when he suddenly snatched a pistol from his pocket and, before anyone could stop him, placed the muzzle within three feet of his victim's head and squeezed the trigger. The bullet from the heavy .45-calibre Colt, serial No. 2079, crashed through Wild Bill's head, coming out through the centre of the right cheek. But before it had spent its force it struck Captain Massey in the left arm, shattering the bone, and became so firmly embedded it had to be cut out. Captain Massey was crippled for life as a result of the shot that killed Wild Bill Hickok.

Bill's reflexes were so phenomenally fast that his hands instinctively reached for his weapons and clutched the butts. He actually had his right-hand gun half out of its holster when he crashed forward, face downward across the table, dead. The five cards he had held in his hand fluttered to the floor: the Ace of Spades, the Ace of Clubs, and the two black Eights, Clubs and Spades. The odd card? The Queen of Hearts!

Until that day the hand was simply referred to as 'Aces and Eights', since the identity of the fifth card was unknown. This piece of information was obtained from Neil Christy, whose father was a friend of Hickok and who was in the saloon when Bill was killed. Mr. Christy's story agrees substantially with what has already been related. He further stated that after the crowd had left the saloon, and Hickok's body had been removed, Carl Mann asked Christy's father to help him clean up the place. It was then that Mr. Christy saw all five of the cards that had fallen to the floor. He kept them for many years and passed them on to his son. But in the course of time they disappeared. So ends the story of the original Dead Man's Hand.

McCall, realizing the enormity of his deed, and half crazy with fear, drove the crowd before him out of the saloon; then ran out of the front door, snapping his pistol at the bartender. Deadwood was quickly ablaze with excitement, and the cry went up all over town: 'Wild Bill has been killed!'

McCall backed away up Main Street, holding a pistol in each hand to keep at bay a large posse of excited citizens. Then he crept into the butcher's shop and hid behind one of the meat-cutting blocks. It is claimed by some that Calamity Jane chased McCall around Shuddey's shop with a meat cleaver, but there is no foundation to this story. Calamity Jane herself stated that it was not true. By no means was Calamity Jane a paramour of Bill Hickok, although recently discovered records indicate they were actually married for a short while. But Bill left her, for, as he later stated, he was ashamed of her. Later Jane emphatically denied that Bill had been her sweetheart, and we cannot blame her for that.

Jack McCall was finally overpowered and captured, and brought back to the scene of the killing. He was held under heavy guard to await disposition of the case. Within an hour the whole of Deadwood was seething with excitement. Threats of lynching were freely and openly expressed.

After McCall's capture and a brief examination at the saloon where he was questioned, he was removed to a building at the lower part of town and a guard placed over him. A coroner's jury was empanelled, with G. H. Sheldon as foreman. After meeting, it rendered a verdict in accordance with the evidence: 'That the deceased, Wild Bill Hickok, had come to his death at the hands of Jack McCall, the result of a shot fired from a pistol, through the back of Wild Bill's head.'

Immediately upon receiving the coroner's verdict preparations were made to bring McCall to trial. McDaniel's Theatre was chosen as the place to hold the proceedings. The citizens of Deadwood held a mass meeting, at which Judge W. L. Kuykendall was chosen to preside at McCall's trial.

It opened on Thursday, August 3, 1876, at two p.m. McCall took a seat to the right of Judge Kuykendall. He presented a most forbidding appearance. McCall was about twenty-seven years old, but dissipation made him appear ten years older. His brow was low and retreating, suggesting a low order of intelligence. His sandy hair, small straggling moustache, and one crossed eye completed the suggestion of a villainous character.

After the jurors had been selected and sworn, the taking of evidence began. It revealed the wantonness of the killing. There was no provocation and no motive, except possibly a love of notoriety to be gained, as McCall thought. At the conclusion of the evidence, McCall was asked if he had anything to say. He leaped to his feet and shouted: 'Yes, you danged right I've got plenty to say. Years ago at Rock Creek that killer Hickok killed my younger brother Andy with a hoe. I swore then and there that I'd kill Wild Bill for it, and I have. I've been following him around for years just waiting for the right chance.'

The trial was concluded about six o'clock, when jury retired to deliberate on a verdict. After an hour and thirty minutes, under the foremanship of Charles Whitehead, they filed back into the improvised courtroom and took their seats. The crowded theatre building was overflowing with spectators as the judge rapped for order.

'Gentlemen of the jury, have you reached a verdict?'

'We have, your honour,' replied Foreman Whitehead.

'Will you please hand your verdict to the clerk, who will read it?' instructed Judge Kuykendall.

The clerk took the folded paper and read slowly as his eyes widened in surprise: 'We, the jury, find the prisoner, Jack McCall, not guilty!'

There was a moment of intense silence; then gradually a low growling, like an angry bulldog's, was heard. The judge rapped for order.

'The bench wishes to warn the spectators there will be no demonstration. The verdict has been rendered by a jury of your own choosing, and whether right or wrong, it is not for me to say.' He

38

paused for a moment, and then said in a rather disgusted tone: 'Prisoner dismissed.'

Immediately Colonel May, who had been appointed prosecuting attorney in the case, flew into a paroxysm of wrath. He called the jurors all the unpleasant names his eloquent tongue could bring to mind. He accused them of selling out, and said he could prove that several thousand ounces of gold dust had been given them to render a 'not guilty' verdict for the hired assassin, as he called McCall. He declared that he would follow McCall's trail until justice was done.

The townspeople buried Wild Bill the next day on the side of a hill now known as Ingleside. His pall-bearers were Bill Hillman, John Oyster, Charley Rich, Jerry Lewis, Charles Young, and Tom Dosier. After the brief ceremonies his old friend, Charlie Utter, wrote on the slab that was placed at the head of his grave:

WILD BILL

J. B. HICKOK

KILLED BY THE ASSASSIN

JACK McCALL

DEADWOOD CITY

BLACK HILLS

August 2, 1876

Pard, we will meet again in the happy

hunting grounds to part no more.

GOODBYE

Colorado Charlie

C. H. Utter

Hickok's body was first buried in a graveyard near where the Fourth Ward school building is now located. Four years later J. S. McClintock assisted the undertaker and two others in exhuming the rough coffin and removing it to Mount Moriah Cemetery. They were astounded to find that, by some natural embalming process of the soil-permeated water which had percolated through the coffin, the body of Wild Bill had been so well preserved as to retain even the outlines of his features and the lines of the manifold pleatings in the dress shirt he had worn. This preservation of the body gave rise to the report that it had been petrified, but Mr. McClintock stated that from his examination he would call it an embalming rather than a petrification, by the disposition of minerals in the tissues of the body.

The admiring people of Deadwood did not forget Wild Bill quickly. For several years following his death wild flowers were placed daily on his grave. Could Calamity Jane have been responsible for this touching attention?

When Bill's wife came to Deadwood to remove his body to Cheyenne she saw how much the grave meant to the people of the town, and changed her mind. She left Deadwood and did not return.

As for Jack McCall, as soon as he was released from custody he left the Black Hills, knowing full well that the friends of Wild Bill would be seeking revenge. He went to Laramie City, Wyoming, and there, while drunk, bragged how he had killed the world's greatest gunman. He felt safe. He couldn't be tried twice for the same crime, so he thought. But he was in a locality where constituted law prevailed, and where the kind of verdict customary at that time in a Black Hills miners' court was not considered legal. He was taken at his own word about the killing of Wild Bill, was arrested and sent to Yankton, the capital of the old Dakota Territory, to stand fresh trial.

Jack McCall was without friends, and so the court appointed General W. H. Beadle and Oliver Shannon as attorneys to defend him. They contended that the crime had been committed in a lawless region wholly outside the jurisdiction of the court. They were overruled.

McCall's trial in the United States District Court began on November 27, 1876, and continued for several days.

McCall gave high tribute to Hickok when he answered this question: 'Why didn't you go around in front of Wild Bill and shoot him in the face like a man?'

'I didn't want to commit suicide,' was his sober reply.

He was convicted and found guilty of murder in the first degree. An appeal was taken to the Supreme Court of the United States, but the finding of the lower court was affirmed, and on January 3, 1877, McCall was sentenced to be hanged on March 1.

On February 21 McCall sent the following note to the local Yankton newspapers:

Editors *Press* and *Dakotaian:*

Sirs: I intend to write an article which I wish your paper, after my death, would publish. If you will be here the day of the execution I will hand it to you. If you accept, or decline, to publish it, let me know.

40

He prepared the article, but on the evening before his execution tore it to bits. That it would have thrown some light on his motive for killing Hickok, and explained his irresponsibility, was the common consensus of opinion.

Under the date of March 1, 1877, one Yankton newspaper carried the following:

At half-past nine, everything being in readiness, the condemned man bade farewell to his fellow prisoners, and left his prison house for the last time. The mournful train, bearing its living victim to the grave, was preceded and followed by a long line of vehicles of every description, with hundreds on horseback and on foot, all leading north, out through Broadway. Not a word was spoken during the ride of two miles to the school section north of the Catholic Cemetery.[1] McCall continued to bear up bravely, even after the gallows loomed in full view.

As soon as possible, after reaching the place, the prisoner mounted the platform of the gallows, accompanied by Deputy Marshal Ash. Here he evinced the same firmness and nerve that had always characterized him since his arrest and trial. He placed himself in the centre of the platform, facing east, and gazed out over the throng, without even a quiver of the lip. U.S. Marshal Burdick, Deputy Ash, Rev. Father Daxacher and his assistant, Mr. Curry, were the only other parties upon the platform.

Immediately the limbs of the unfortunate culprit were pinioned, when he knelt with his spiritual adviser. Turning his face toward heaven, his lips were seen to move in prayer. Upon rising he kissed the crucifix; and after the black cap had been placed over his head, the U.S. Marshal placed the noose around his neck. He then said: 'Wait one moment, Marshal, until I pray.'

Marshal Burdick waited until he had uttered a prayer, and then adjusted the noose, when McCall said: 'Draw it tighter, Marshal.'

All was now in readiness; and the assemblage of nearly one thousand persons seemed to hold their breath. It was an awful moment—the single step between life and death. At precisely 10.15 a.m. the trap was sprung and with the single choking expression, 'Oh, God!' uttered while the drop fell, the body of John McCall was dangling between heaven and earth.

So the last chapter was written, and Jack McCall joined James Butler Hickok in eternity.

---

[1] Where the scaffold had been erected, and near where the South Dakota State Hospital for the Insane now stands.

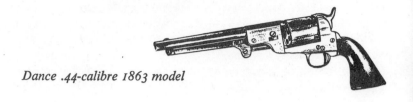

Dance .44-calibre 1863 model

2 Wild Bill Longley

WILLIAM PRESTON LONGLEY was nurtured in the South's blackest moment, lived hard, died young, and fought his own personal version of the Civil War right up to the day he walked to the gallows, thirteen years after Appomattox. He left behind a record of wanton, wholesale murder seldom equalled in the history of the West. During his brief but boisterous lifetime he put thirty-two men in their graves, counting Negroes and Mexicans.

At one time in his almost charmed life he rode reckless and wild through the State of Texas while every law officer was on his trail, and both the United States Government and the Governor put a price on his head. He once cheated a hangman's noose in a fashion so bizarre it would be laughed off if it appeared in a piece of fiction. For half of his twenty-seven years he seemed so invincible that when he did walk up to the noose for the last time more than four thousand people crowded around the gallows to see the sight. To this day there are those who earnestly believe that the ruthless killer framed his own hanging, and escaped to South America on that October day in 1878 when he supposedly met his Maker.

This was Wild Bill Longley. Cold-blooded, vicious, psychopathic. The only good thing that can be said of him is that he died young, and most of those who knew him thought that wasn't soon enough. He began life as a nineteenth-century juvenile delinquent, was a dead shot before he was fifteen, and a killer before most lads his age were out of high school.

Wild Bill Longley

* Longley was born October 16, 1851, in Austin County, Texas, along Mill Creek. He was the son of Campbell Longley, a devout, God-fearing, hard-working man., The Longley family moved to Evergreen in Lee County when Bill was two years old. At this time Evergreen was still a part of Washington County. It was a place familiar to the older Longley. Not more than a mile away was the San Antonio–Nacogdoches Road, the Camino Real, and the monument to the valiant Texans who fought against Santa Ana in the Mexican War. Campbell Longley had been one of them. He had shown valour and courage above and beyond the call of duty at San Jacinto. He was a proud Texan and his son inherited that pride. Young Bill might never have embarked on his terrifying career of murder had it not been for the time and place he occupied in Texan history.

Longley was fourteen when the Civil War ended and when living in Texas became a nightmare existence. In the wake of the Confederate surrender Texas became a land of outrage and humiliation, overrun with scallywags, carpet-baggers, crooked politicians, and Negroes anxious to test their newly won freedom as 'police officers' in a place which had once held them in slavery and servitude. Vandalism and viciousness became as common as the noonday sun. The Texas Rangers had been disbanded, and in their place ruled the State Police, controlled by ruthless opportunists with armed Negro soldiers at their backs.

However, it was not long before the corrupt police had to replace the firearms in the hands of the coloured militants. They substituted a lead ball attached to a stout leather thong, the forerunner of the blackjack, and a brutal weapon when used as a bludgeon. The rule of the State Police was a humiliating experience for men like Campbell Longley, and his young son was quick to feel the hatred which boiled up inside the broken Confederates.

At fourteen Longley was a boy large for his age, whose schooling had included little more than learning to read and write. What he learned outside the classroom, however, he learned well. By the time he reached his fourteenth birthday Bill was an accomplished marksman who could put six shots into an oak-tree in an area the size of a dinner plate while riding past at breakneck speed. Such shooting was done with his father's antiquated percussion-cap revolver. For the

43

calling Longley was eventually to follow, this was all the schooling he needed.

It was in such a climate of hate, fear, oppression, and degeneration that Longley quickly matured, a bitter, resentful youth with a volcanic temper. It was inevitable that he should put his pistol to use against the society he hated. The clash came in Houston, ironically at a time when Bill Longley had run off to the city to obtain a good Colt revolver, a prize he had yearned for since he first fired his father's outmoded pistol.

He hopped a Texas and Houston freight train and leaped off as it slid to a halt in Houston on a cold, rainy day in 1866. Friendless, he spent his first night huddled around a common camp-fire blazing in the square, and listening to the older men discussing the tragedy of the times. The next day he struck up a friendship with a youth several years his senior, and that night he experienced his first brush with violence. It came in a windswept alley while the two youths sought a place to spend the night. A burly Negro in the blue uniform of the Union Army, swinging a lead ball at his side, blocked their path and demanded to know their names and their business. Then the bully demanded that they undress in the street in the bitter cold. When they hesitated he charged at them, swinging his lead mace. Longley's companion pulled a Bowie knife from under his shirt and struck swiftly, burying the blade deep in the Negro's side.

Both boys knew the consequences of killing a Negro policeman. They parted company, and the next day Bill was back in Evergreen, sporting a Dance six-shooter, the gun made famous by the Confederacy during the recent war. He didn't bother to explain where he got it, and nobody asked. Now Billy Longley was happy—he had two pistols. Many writers have claimed that a two-gun gunman was a creature of legend, that using two pistols simultaneously to advantage was impossible. Young Longley proved an exception to this belief. He could use either hand or both at the same time with equal effect. Many of his friends reported he could empty both guns into a six-inch area at the same time.

It was shortly after his return from Houston that Longley had his first solo clash with the Negroes. A surly coloured man carrying a rifle rode down the Camino Real cursing all white men. As he passed the Longley ranch he called to the older Longley, damning him. Young Bill was nearby. He walked into the front yard and ordered the Negro to throw down his gun. The sullen soldier swung the rifle up and fired a shot at Bill, then switched his horse into a gallop. Longley, firing from a crouch, sent his first shot through the Negro's head. He tossed a rope around the dead man, dragged the body into a shallow ditch, and buried it. The crime was never reported and nobody knew this Negro was Longley's first victim until Bill confessed on the gallows, twelve years later.

One thing, however, can be said for young Longley. In those days of general discontent many armed men turned to outlawry. Longley, as far as is known, never used his guns in a hold-up, although later he was involved in some unsavoury deals.

Bill joined in partnership with another local youth, Johnson McKowen, breaking wild horses for training. Shortly after Bill had killed his first victim, he and McKowen went to Lexington, Texas, to enter one of their horses in a race. They withdrew just before the race when several Negroes also signed up for the run. The two young men well knew that, even if their horse won, their chances of collecting the purse were slim. That night Longley took his revenge against the coloured people. The Negroes were having a dance in the street when Johnson and Bill rode into town. The sixteen-year-old boy spurred his horse to a gallop and rode into the midst of the gathering, firing both guns. Two men were killed and several seriously wounded.

Bill Longley had embarked upon a career which was to earn him the nickname of 'the nigger killer'. His reputation quickly spread throughout the state. Once, while riding on a H. & T.C. Railroad car, Longley fell asleep with his feet in the aisle. A new Negro porter ordered him to pull in his legs, but Longley ignored him. The porter forcibly pushed Longley's feet back. Then he boastfully explained to the conductor that he had just 'showed some white trash a thing or two'. When the conductor told him the man was Wild Bill Longley the porter jumped off the train.

Early in his youth Longley seems to have developed a mean streak that was more than just a hatred for Negroes. In 1868 a circus made one of its rare appearances in Evergreen. It was a holiday for the town, since there was little recreation in the small village. Longley and one of his chums went to the main tent and demanded

45

free admittance. When the owner refused the arrogant Longley slugged him unconscious and entered the tent, where he forced two clowns to dance a fast jig while he fired shots at their feet. His performance started a near panic. The spectators left on the run, and the show quickly folded its tents and left town. That was the last time that particular circus ever appeared in Evergreen.

Before he was eighteen Longley had become a self-appointed champion of the white man's cause. One night three heavily armed Negroes rode into Evergreen and entered the bar. They demanded drinks and boasted they had heard Evergreen was unfavourable to men of their race, and they were there to see just how tough it really was. Nobody offered resistance, but someone quickly got word to Longley. Young Bill came into town on the run. His intention, he said, was merely to disarm the three, to show them who was boss. By the time Bill got to the bar the boasters were gone. Longley followed them into Burleson County, about ten miles from Evergreen, and rode into their camp. He had no time to utter a word before one of the Negroes pulled a gun and took a shot at the white youth. Before the Negro had a chance to get his second shot off Longley put a bullet squarely between the man's eyes. The other two Negroes threw down their guns and ran. This killing put the law on Longley's trail.

On Christmas Day 1868, a few days after he shot the Negro in Burleson County, friends warned Bill that law officers were on their way to arrest him. The young killer knew he wouldn't stand much chance in a Yankee courtroom, so he left home on the run. He got a job working for John Reagan, a large stock owner in Karnes County, which was then the scene of a bitter cattle feud between the Taylor and Sutton families. Soldiers had been called in to settle the range war. Although Longley took no active part in the struggle, he was a close friend of the Taylor family. While riding through Yorktown one day, Longley was mistaken for Charles Taylor. The Army had been ordered to arrest members of both families in an attempt to end the feud, and they went after Bill. Not realizing it was a case of mistaken identity when some soldiers approached him, Longley thought they were after him for the Burleson shooting. He made a run for it, outdistancing all but the sergeant, who raced his horse close in beside Longley and yelled to him to surrender. Longley

46

pulled his pistol, jammed it into the sergeant's side and killed him with one shot—the last one he had in his pistol. Fortune had begun to ride with Bill Longley.

With the Army now at his heels, Bill returned to Evergreen, but his father insisted that the youth would not be safe there. He persuaded Longley to join forces with Cullen Montgomery Baker, who led a band of renegades and outlaws which constantly harassed the Yankees.

Longley went to the headquarters of the daring guerilla in Bowie County, but learned that Baker was in Arkansas. While awaiting his return, Bill met and befriended a local youth named Tom Johnson. Unknown to Longley, Johnson was a wanted horse thief. Bill accompanied young Johnson to his home to spend the night, but before dawn a band of vigilantes surrounded the Johnson house and dragged both boys into the yard. Without ceremony they carried the youths to a nearby tree and lynched them. Wheeling their horses, the posse rode out of the yard. As they passed the two swaying bodies they fired several shots at them. Luck was still smiling at Longley. One bullet struck Bill's heavy belt buckle and glanced off without injuring him. A second snipped the rope from which he was hanging and frayed it. Then the rope snapped, and Longley fell unconscious to the ground. He might have strangled had not Johnson's younger brother quickly pulled the rope from around his neck. Nothing could be done for Johnson. He was dead.

Suffering from shock, Longley hid in the brush near the Johnson home to recuperate. The Johnsons provided him with clothing and food, and passed the word to Cullen Baker of the Johnson-Longley hanging. Baker returned to Texas shortly afterwards and invited Bill to join his gang.

Little is known about Cullen Baker's renegades except that they never robbed people of Southern sympathies. They looted Government trains and protected friends from carpet-baggers and grafting tax collectors, often turning over their loot to poor Southerners, much the same as did the Jameses and Youngers when they first began their outlaw careers. Baker's career was shortlived. He was hunted down and killed in 1869, a year after Bill Longley joined the gang. Bill returned to Evergreen after Baker's death. It has been estimated that while with Baker young Longley killed seven men, not counting several Negroes shot to death by members of the group collectively. In Evergreen Longley struck terror in the hearts of the Negro residents. Carrying on his strange and frightening vendetta, he killed eight more coloured men before leaving on a trip to visit kinsmen in Utah.

By now Longley's unrelenting death rampage was beginning to tell on the youth's mind. Blood-letting came to him naturally, and he killed at the slightest provocation. On his way to Utah, he joined a trail herd owned by a cattleman named Rector, who was driving his cattle from Bee County, Texas, to Kansas. Rector was as mean in temperament as was Longley, and abused his hands viciously. Bill was quick to criticize Rector's actions, and the cowman, believing he had an easy mark in a seventeen-year-old boy, invited Longley to step out and settle things with revolvers. Bill quickly accepted the challenge. Man and boy walked out on to the prairie, but before Rector could clear leather he was dead. Bill shot him six times before the man hit the ground.

After the death of Rector, Longley left the camp with a cowpoke named Davis, heading for Abilene. They stopped at a general store for a drink, and were told by the proprietor that a posse was nearby chasing two horse thieves. While Longley and Davis were still in the store, two men named McClelland and Shelley entered, ordered whisky, and openly bragged they were riding stolen horses. Longley thought over their boast, and the next day rode into their trail camp and arrested them both at gunpoint. The bold young killer led both men back to Abilene and collected a reward.

However, Longley didn't remain long in the Kansas cattle town. Marshal Tom Smith had a standing order that no firearms could be worn in town. Longley, whose reputation was beginning to grow, knew if he took off his guns his life would be worthless. He left his friend Davis in Abilene and headed for Leavenworth. The gunfighter pattern was now beginning to weave itself inexplicably around Wild Bill Longley. He had chosen to make the six-gun his career, and it now became his role to prove his prowess with the pistol at every provocation. While drinking in a saloon in Leavenworth one night he overheard a soldier say: 'Well, if I were from Texas I'd keep it to myself, and be too ashamed to admit it.'

Longley is recorded as replying: 'There are a lot of honest, fine people in Texas. You can't judge all people there by the likes of me and others of outlaw breed.'

The young trooper fancied himself quite a gunman, and chose to make an issue of the comment. It was his last mistake. He remarked there wasn't an honest man in Texas and that the women were no good. Without further argument Longley drew and shot the trooper dead. He escaped, but instead of taking a horse and heading for the brush Bill hopped a freight for St. Louis. A telegraph message tripped him up. He was captured as the train went through St. Joseph and was returned to Leavenworth's military prison. Oddly enough, the Army never realized the man they had in custody was wanted throughout half of Texas. Bill was charged only with the shooting of the soldier, and after he had been held for several weeks a prison guard informed him that he was to be shot within a few days. Longley offered the guard fifty dollars, which he had hidden in his shoes, in exchange for freedom. The guard quickly took him up on the proposition. Once again he escaped death by a hair.

With the dragnet for him widening like a puddle in the rain, Longley decided to go north, this time into Indian country. From Leavenworth he made Cheyenne and joined a party of miners who were going into the dread Big Horn Mountains, a dangerous and foolhardy mission—125 white men into a section alive with Sioux war parties, all of them ready to kill. The party had several brushes with old Spotted Tail, one of the Sioux chieftains, but managed to battle their way along the Wind River to Camp Brown. Several men were lost, but the mining party had with it several field-pieces. Had it not been for the destructive power of the cannon, the entire party would probably have lost their scalps.

At Camp Brown they were ordered to abandon the expedition, since it was a violation of General Grant's treaty with Chief Red Cloud for white men to enter the Black Hills and Big Horn Mountain country. Ignoring the order, the group headed into the Black Hills, followed by five companies of soldiers with orders to bring them back peacefully or otherwise. The miners ran headlong into another skirmish with the Indians, and although they managed to fight off the attacking redskins, the Army companies ran them down. At the threat of a court-martial, they finally turned back to the fort.

Young Longley, although he hated the idea of working for the

Yankees, realized he was safe at the Army camp, and took a job as a teamster. It was during the following winter that luck once again smiled on Wild Bill Longley. While on a hunting trip in the mountains, Bill and several friends were trapped in a violent blizzard. Three of the men froze to death in the icy blasts, but Longley dragged himself back to the camp, more dead than alive. For three months he was unable to walk. When Bill regained his health he was given charge of the Government corrals. That brought him the responsibility of taking care of the packhorses and mules.

The unscrupulous Texan was approached shortly by Quartermaster Greggory, a crooked scoundrel who was fleecing the Government in the transactions of horses and supplies. The two were birds of a feather, and Longley unhesitatingly agreed to Greggory's scheme —that the two men would collaborate, out-count the Army of its horseflesh, and sell the animals they could come by illegally at a clear profit. Longley, however, had a wider streak of crookedness than Greggory. He sold the first two mules the men embezzled for five hundred dollars and told Greggory he received three hundred. The crooked quartermaster had contacts of his own. He learned Longley was cheating him out of his agreed share and threatened to kill him.

Bill and Greggory seem to have reached a friendly understanding about the other two hundred dollars, but Greggory returned to his rooms and brooded about his partner's double dealing. He went armed to the corral to give his young partner a lesson. Bill saw him coming. When Greggory walked into the corral Longley stepped from behind a post and shot him down before he could draw his gun. Greggory died the next day, but Longley didn't wait for his demise. He mounted a slow-moving mule and headed for the brush again. Three days later the Army caught up with him and he was returned to the stockade.

Nine months passed before he was tried; during which time Longley escaped once and was recaptured. He was eventually tried and sentenced to death, but the sentence was commuted, and Bill received thirty years in the Iowa State Prison. Before he could be transferred from the post he again broke out of the stockade, and this time made for Indian country. The Army authorities did not follow. Longley insured his escape by taking up residence with the Ute Indians for nearly a year. It was apparently an experience

Longley enjoyed more than any other in his entire life. Although homesickness finally got the better of him, and he left his Indian friends to return to Texas, Bill often spoke of his life with the Utes and described his experiences with them.

On the way from Iowa to Texas he got in a card game with a young man named Charles Stuart of Parkersville, Kansas. An argument started and the hot-headed Longley used his gun again, shooting Stuart to death at the card table. Stuart's father quickly posted a fifteen-hundred-dollar reward for the return of his son's slayer, known to Kansans as Tom Jones. Always the conniver, Longley contacted two local outlaws and agreed to allow them to turn him over to the sheriff for the reward if they would then break him out of jail. The outlaws agreed, Longley was turned over to the law, thrown into jail, and the reward money was paid to Longley's co-conspirators. Next day the two outlaws entered the unsuspecting sheriff's office on the pretext of wanting to speak to Longley, overpowered the lawman, and freed Bill. The three men split the fifteen hundred dollars, and Longley continued his journey south. As usual, the gunman's luck had held. The outlaws could just as easily have left him to his fate and split the reward two ways.

Bill Longley returned to his father's farm in Bell County, and for several months kept out of trouble, doing farm chores and caring for the ranch. With a thousand-dollar price on his head, however, Longley couldn't keep out of sight of the law for very long. When a posse was formed in Lee County to go and arrest him, a friend raced to the ranch and warned Bill. Longley took a Colt revolver and a fast horse, and rode to Comanche County, to hide out with friends. While performing an errand one afternoon he learned that a Negro had insulted the wife of a man named W. Forsythe, and forced her to cook his dinner and feed his horse. Longley followed the man into town. There the Negro faced Longley, pushed his hat back on his head, and demanded: 'Who the hell are you?'

Longley's answer was two .45 slugs through the arrogant coloured man's brain. Riding west from the scene of the shooting, Bill was overtaken by a five-man posse as he entered the Santa Anna Mountain range. Racing into the mountain underbrush, Longley killed one of his pursuers and sent the rest hightailing back to where they had come from.

Despite the constant efforts of the law to run him down and bring him to justice, Longley continued to keep ahead of his would-be captors. In Madison County he actually befriended a sheriff. Although he was using the assumed name of William Henry, Sheriff Finley recognized Longley from descriptive 'wanted' dodgers. He carefully planned to gain Bill's confidence, then trap him. Bill, however, was also alert and suspicious of Finley's friendship. On the night Finley planned to arrest the gunslinger a game of cards was arranged. The sheriff had two men staked out at the meeting-place. Longley didn't show up. He had fled to Gillespie County, there to meet several friends in a bar and plan another card game. An informant in the group warned Finley. A second trap was planned. And for the second time Longley eluded the lawmen, this time riding towards Kerrville.

Finley was not to be denied, however. He followed the wily Texan and surprised Bill at his camp the next morning. Finley showed Longley a warrant for arrest, and promised him safe conduct back to Austin. Longley's fame as a killer was so widespread by this time that crowds gathered all along the route, trying to tear off pieces of his clothing, seeking a lock of his hair, or just bunching up along the road for a look at the youthful badman.

Longley's fabulous luck held again. In Austin Governor E. J. Davis, who had offered the reward for Longley's capture, had lost the election to Richard Coke. The new Governor refused to take Bill into custody. Finley, who was only interested in the reward money, had Longley on his hands and wasn't quite sure what to do with him. William Patterson, a cousin of Longley, solved the dilemma. He offered Finley 563 dollars for Bill's release. It was the best offer Finley got, and he took it. Longley went scot-free.

Bill wasn't loose long before a Mexican from Frio County fell victim to his fast draw and unerring aim. The Mexican had made the mistake of selling Longley a stolen horse. Travelling to Bandera County, Bill secured a job on the Wadkins Ranch and settled to hard, honest work. But his fame caught up with him before he became too firmly enamoured of law and order. He had struck up a friendship with a man named Will Scrier from a neighbouring ranch. Scrier turned out to be as unscrupulous and cold-blooded as Bill. Before long both men were suspicious of each other. Longley learned that Scrier, whose real name was Lew Sawyer, planned to turn him over to the sheriff for a new reward Bill's capture carried. He beat Scrier to the punch. Longley told the local Justice of the Peace that Scrier was a desperate and savage man wanted by the law and offered to capture him. The Justice deputized Longley, and with a young man named Hayes the crafty gunfighter went after Scrier.

They arrived at Scrier's quarters at night and Longley realized that the victim would be suspicious if he was summoned from his home after dark without good reason, so he called out and told his prey that he had a side of beef down the road. He offered Scrier a share. The unsuspecting man came out and joined the two riders. As they rode down the path from Scrier's home, Longley fell back and drew, ordering Scrier to surrender.

The other gunman proved more of an opponent than Bill had bargained for. Pulling his pistol, he fired a shot over his shoulder and tried to make a break. Bill shot him under the right shoulder. Scrier kept going, firing behind him as he dashed down the glade. Hayes' horse shied and darted off into the brush, but Bill was determined to complete the fight, one way or another. He followed hard on Scrier's trail, putting four more bullets into his adversary's back. Scrier finally wheeled his horse in a tight turn, pulled his shotgun, and fired a blast at the oncoming Longley. Bill's horse plunged dead to the ground. The two men opened fire at close range, and Scrier was hit several more times. Still he kept up the bitter fight. Finally Longley swung into an advantageous position and caught Scrier squarely between the eyes. The man rolled over dead. When Longley checked, there were thirteen bullets in Scrier's body. He later said that Scrier was the hardest man to kill he had ever met. Mounting Scrier's horse, Bill rode back into Uvalde, told the Justice that Scrier was dead and resigned his commission. It was one of the shortest deputy commissions on record, and in his own peculiar way Longley had actually performed a service for the law.

During this period Bill continued to hold his terrifying grudge against the Negroes. Once in Logansport he heard a Negro had insulted an elderly white man. He simply rode up to the Negro's house, called him out, and shot him to death. In Angelina County he was riding along and came on a Negro and a white man fighting in the middle of the road. Bill ended the fight by killing the Negro.

In April 1875 Longley committed the crime which was to bring about his demise. Bill had been working on the farm of William Baker on Walnut Creek, in Bastrop County. His brother was working on the same ranch, and Bill managed to keep in contact with the rest of his family for the first time in years. Soon after coming to the Baker ranch he learned that a cousin, Cale Longley, was dead.There were two stories concerning Cale's death. Some said he had been killed by Wilson Anderson, a boyhood friend of Bill. Anderson, however, claimed that Cale had fallen off his horse and died as a result of injuries suffered in the fall. In most quarters Cale's death was accepted as an accident, but the dead man's father stubbornly stuck to the claim that Anderson had killed his son.

One Saturday morning Bill's brother told him that Sheriff Jim Brown of Lee County was on his way to the Baker place to arrest him. Longley revealed to the Baker family his true identity, and left, riding straight to his cousin's ranch. Cale Longley's father repeated the story that Wilson Anderson was responsible for Cale's death, knowing full well that Bill would wreak swift vengeance for the death of his relative. He was right. Longley rode to the farm of Wilson Anderson the morning of April 1, 1875. Anderson, ploughing a field, looked up to see Bill Longley riding towards him, a shotgun cradled in his arm. Before Anderson could say a word, Longley cut him down with the vicious weapon.

Mortally wounded, Anderson gasped: 'Oh, God, what did you shoot me for, Bill?'

'Just for luck,' Longley replied.

The death of Anderson might have gone unsolved had it not been for Longley's penchant for bragging. There were no witnesses, but Bill later described the killing to Wash Harris at his father's ranch. Three years later Longley heard his words repeated, this time at the trial which was to result in his hanging.

A few months after the Anderson murder Longley secured a job under the name of Jim Patterson at the farm of Captain Sedbury. Apparently happy with his job as a farmhand, Bill put in over ten hours a day working the cotton machinery and other implements on the farm. Following a foxhunt and race at the Sedbury farm, however, Longley got into a trivial argument with George Thomas, a local bully and braggart. A fist fight followed, and there probably

54

would have been a shooting had not Sedbury disarmed the two men. When Thomas finally left for the night Sedbury returned Longley's gun to him, thinking the matter was over. But Bill Longley's temper was far from soothed. He followed Thomas into town, waited while he awoke a storekeeper, Frank Jones, and bought a bottle of whisky, and then, while the two men stood on the porch of the store, Bill·rode by. Thomas saw him coming and went for his gun, but Longley was much too fast. Only one shot was fired, and Thomas was lying dead on the doorstep. Once again Longley was on the run.

On February 12, 1876, while working as a woodcutter near Crockett, Texas, Bill stopped at a bleak farmhouse near the town of Ben Franklin, in Delta County. There he met and fell in love with Louvenia Jacks. Contemporary newspapers gave this as the statement Bill made after he met the Texas beauty:

It was there I met the first girl I ever loved, and never on earth will forget the feeling of my heart the moment I laid eyes on her, and I never will be ashamed to acknowledge that I did love her with all my heart. It was on the 12th day of February in 1876 that I met her. I introduced myself as William Black of Missouri and had lived in Texas for three years, I said. We sat up late that night and I related many of my adventures, all of which the beautiful girl listened to with great interest. The family was composed of old man Jacks, his wife, and two grown daughters, Jennie and Louvenia, the last named the younger, and it was her with whom I fell madly in love.

Bill immediately made arrangements to work for a preacher named Roland Lay on a sharing basis. The Lay farm was only a mile from the Jacks place, and the girl's family seemed to like Bill. Shortly afterwards Longley learned that Louvenia had another suitor, a man who had the reputation of being a badman. He was Roland Lay's cousin. Naturally the Lay family wanted their kinsman to win Lou's hand, and did everything possible to discourage Longley's courtship. When the local townsfolk heard about the 'Mister Black' who was also courting the pretty girl, they assumed that the hired hand was marked for a quick grave.

Longley received several threatening notes and traced them back to Preacher Lay. He accused the reverend gentleman of trying to beat him out of his share of the crops. Lay immediately paid off

55

Bill's share and Longley left. Instead of moving on, however, he hired out to a farmer, near Paris, in nearby Lamar County, and continued his courtship with Louvenia. The embittered Lay swore out a warrant against Longley, charging that Bill had threatened his life. Bill, as William Black, was arrested at once and lodged in the Cooper jail. Since he had no one to pay his bond he visualized months, perhaps years, as a prisoner. In desperation he set fire to the jail and escaped.

Astride his own horse, Bill rode to the Jacks farm, secured a shotgun, and made his way to the Lay farm. Lay was in the cowpen, his shotgun standing against the fence. Longley later described what happened:

I walked into the cowpen and stood between him and his gun. He looked up and saw me and turned white as a sheet. He seemed to know that his time had come and that he would get no mercy at my hands. When he saw me I told him it was the last of 'pea time' with him, and if he had anything to say he had better be at it. He said he hated to die and leave his wife and family. Then I asked him why he did not let me alone when I was at peace with him and all his kinsfolk. To this he gave no answer and I dropped my gun to level with his body and fired. The gun was heavily loaded with turkey shot. He fell backwards and I left him.

On June 23, 1876, Governor Richard Coke of Texas offered a reward of five hundred dollars for the arrest and delivery inside the jail doors of Delta County, Texas, of one William Black, alias William Longley, for the murder of Roland Lay, a minister. Things had changed in Texas. The newly elected Governor had disbanded the Negro police and thrown out the State Police. The Texas Rangers had replaced them, and law and order in the state was returning. Thousands of 'Joe Doe' warrants had been issued, and the Rangers were rounding up suspects by the hundreds. Many arrested on suspicion of one crime were indicted and convicted for other crimes they had committed. The Governor doubled the reward for Longley, whose description was telegraphed throughout the state. Longley knew now that Texas was no longer a safe place for him. With the Rangers on his trail it would only be a matter of time before he was arrested. He fled across the border into Louisiana and rented land near Keatchie, in De Soto Parish.

Longley was no fool. He rented the land from the sheriff, who later said that Bill showed great signs of making money and becoming a prosperous farmer. In the months that followed Longley courted and became engaged to the lawman's daughter, settled down, and appeared to be a law-abiding, hard-working citizen. He also befriended a young constable named Courtney and they became good friends.

Longley, in his apparently earnest desire to change his life, offered to help Courtney in his official duties, and in so doing inadvertently tipped his hand. Courtney began wondering how this stranger knew so many angles in the law business; slowly he began to suspect that Bill was not just a farmer. He discussed the matter with the sheriff. At first the sheriff refused to believe there was anything suspicious about the young man engaged to his daughter. Then for some unknown reason Longley revealed his true identity to the girl. Courtney and the girl's father contacted Sheriff Milton Mast of Nacogdoches, who rushed to the sheriff's home with Deputy Sheriff W. M. Burroughs. Bill was working in the fields with a revolver in his pocket. Mast and Burroughs hid in the shadows of the house, and when Longley came in from the fields the officers stepped out with cocked shotguns and ordered him to surrender. Longley stated later he could do nothing but give up in the face of the wicked-looking shotguns. Sheriff Mast never bothered to take out extradition papers, he was only ten miles from the Texas border. He hurried his prisoner across the border to Henderson and the next day took Longley into Giddings, Texas.

Longley was taken into custody on May 13, 1877, and a report of his arrest appeared on June 27 in the Panola, Texas, *Watchman*:

On yesterday evening Captain Milt Mast of Nacogdoches County and W. M. Burroughs of the same county, arrived in Henderson, having under arrest one William Longley, a notorious murderer of Lee County, Texas. Captain Mast was corresponding with friends in Lee County and by this means got on the track of the desperado. He and Mr. Burroughs captured the prisoner last Wednesday near Keatchie (De Soto Parish), Louisiana, at a point about ten miles from the Texas line and about twenty miles east of Logansport, La. They will take the train today for Lee County where they intend to deliver him to the proper authorities. A 1,050 dollar reward has been offered for his arrest by different counties. He says he has killed

57

thirty-two men. Captain Mast requests all those counties that have offered rewards for William Longley to come and settle up. Captain Mast was furnished with the following letter from the district clerk of Lee County which suits the description in every particular.

Giddings, Lee County, Texas
May 18, 1877

M. Mast, Esq.,
Nacogdoches, Texas
Dear Sir,

Your esteemed favour of April 24th was received today. Allow me to thank you for your interest in the arrest of criminals. Longley is today the worst man in Texas—he has committed many murders in this vicinity—he has even murdered a woman. He is about six feet high; weighs 150 pounds; tolerably spare build; black hair, eyes, and whiskers; slightly stooped in shoulders. I have been told by those who know him that he can be recognized in a crowd of 100 men by the keenness and blackness of his eyes. There are several large rewards offered for him by citizens, one from this county for $250. He has assumed names. You will have to take advantage of him—he will fight and is a good shot. Please keep me posted—we want him. Our sheriff once followed him to the Louisiana line. Thanking you and tending you all official courtesy that I may be able to render, I am

Very respectfully yours,
W. A. KNOX

Lodged in the Giddings jail, Longley wrote many letters to the Texas newspapers, most of which were published. They give perhaps some insight into this cold-blooded killer's character. In some cases the writings are almost pathetic. Bill was not permitted to write to his relatives, nor were they allowed to visit him. The following letter was written to a Texas newspaper during Longley's incarceration:

Well, the blow is over; the die is cast and I am condemned to die without the sympathy of a single human being that I can recall. You are all eager and hope to see me brought to the scaffold. Then I hope your vengeance will be fully glutted, and that you will all be fully satisfied when you see the last footing from under me and my soul hurled into eternity. Then, folks, for God's sake I hope that prejudice will cease when I pay this dreadful debt which is exacted of me by the law. I am willing to pay this debt for the good of the rising generation, and I hope now, that the law will triumph over all lawless characters, for of course you know my reasoning faculties are good enough to know that the world would run back into barbarism if the laws of the land were not enforced. Certainly, life is sweet; yet I cannot expect to escape the penalty of the law. For, should I escape, either by pardon or by breaking jail, it would be encouraging to all boys that are now growing up and who are disposed to be outlaws. I have two dear brothers who are now in their boyhood, and are disposed to be wilder than I was, and I hope this will be a warning to them, for I would freely die, rather than see them live the life that I have been living, and yet I believe I have been the most successful outlaw that ever lived in Texas, as far back as I can remember.

But look at me now. After all the victories that I have gained over my enemies, the past ten or twelve years, I now sit through the dragging and weary hours of the days and nights, gazing out upon the beautiful earth over which I have roamed free as a bird many a day and hour. Here I sit, now in the felon's cell awaiting the death that I know is certain, and yet out of it all, I am thankful to Almighty God, that I have the opportunity to repent of my sins and fit my soul for the last step that will take my soul into the realms of an unknown future, and also to advise the rising generation and tell them of the evils and dangers of a reckless life. There are many who may not take my advice. If I can be the means of saving only one soul from eternal ruin, it will pay me for all the writing I have done, since I have been in jail. Not for any good that it could do me, nor to boast of my exploits, but only to show the rising generation the great danger and folly of such life, and that those who persist in following such a career overlook the fact that they are liable to be cut down any moment without preparation for the future. I am one of the fortunate ones, who has been blessed with a little time in which to make this preparation, and I think I should devote every moment of time now, to doing good, after having thrown away so much precious time, that I could have put to profitable use. But now it is too late for me, but it is not too late for all young boys who may read this, and who are now blessed with being in possession of a happy home, and have the daily advice of Christian parents, as I once had, but never availed myself of the opportunity.

And now, boys, remember the road Bill Longley had travelled, in disobeying his parents, and when you start to do wrong remember that a very small wrong always leads to still greater ones, and so on until finally, nothing will seem wrong to you if you follow the wrong road. My first step was disobedience; next whisky drinking; next carrying pistols; next gambling, and then murder, and I suppose the next will be the gallows. I hope my father and mother will never be blamed for what I have done for they tried to raise me right.

Signed,

BILL LONGLEY

Bill Longley was tried before Judge E. B. Turner in Giddings on September 3, 1877. The main witness for the state was Wash Harris, who swore that Longley admitted the murder of Wilson Anderson. The trial moved swiftly. The following day the case was argued and given to the jury. It took them an hour and a half to find Bill guilty, and he was sentenced to hang.

Longley apparently never gave up hope of rescue or escape until a few days before the scheduled hanging. The State Supreme Court upheld the decision in an appeal, during which Longley was moved to Galveston, and he was sentenced to die on October 11, 1878. While in Galveston he embraced the Catholic religion and was christened by the Rev. Chambodut. The Rev. Father Spillard of Austin was with Bill the night before and the morning of the hanging.

The day of the execution dawned murky and hot with rain threatening in a leaden sky. A crowd gathered early and by one-thirty p.m. more than four thousand persons were assembled about the gallows, many of them Negroes.

It looked bad, but the authorities had foreseen such a crowd, and had a company of infantry under Captain W. G. McLennan and forty mounted deputies under Captain S. P. Riggleton. Carpenters worked all morning building the gallows, and it was not finished until shortly before one o'clock. All the time hundreds of anxious spectators sat or stood around, waiting for 'the curtain to raise'. As one old-timer put it: 'By golly, you'd think President Hayes himself was visiting Giddings. Effen he was don't think any more folks could get in than come to see Longley die.'

At one-thirty Sheriff Jim Brown and his army went for Longley at the jail. A deep feeling of friendship had developed between Brown and Longley, something akin to a father-and-son under-standing. Brown opened the cell door and found Bill sitting on the bunk. The latter smiled up at the sheriff and greeted him with a wave of his hand.

60

'Howdy, Jim.'

The sheriff took a deep breath and said: 'Well, Bill, it's time to saddle up.' His voice trailed off to a whisper and he avoided Longley's searching eyes.

'I've been listening to them building that contraption,' said Longley, after a moment, 'and I'm curious to see what it looks like. Never saw a real gallows in my life.' He laughed at his joke as he lit a large black cigar.

'Sorry to do this,' mumbled the sheriff, as he fiddled with the chains on Longley's wrists. 'These blamed things are more trouble than anything I ever saw. Sorry I have to use 'em.'

'That's all right, Jim. Come on. I'm anxious to get out of this cage.'

They led Bill outside between the two lines of infantry and guards to a covered wagon. Four guards holding double-barrelled shotguns were seated in the wagon, and Longley took his place in the middle—two guards on each side of him. A fifth guard sat on the seat with the driver. Mounted deputies rode in front and rear and the infantry flanked the vehicle.

Driving through the throng, the wagon was drawn up at the foot of the gallows. Without a moment's hesitation Longley stepped lightly from the wagon to the ground and paused on the bottom step to survey the structure with a critical eye. Then for the first time he seemed to take notice of the heavy guard and the tremendous crowd.

'Expecting a king or something, Sheriff? Anyway, you got a good audience and a regular army too.' With that Bill turned and gazed upon the rope as it dangled from the gibbet.

'The darn thing looks strong enough, all right.' He took a couple of steps up and tested the steps by shaking his weight on it.

'Look out, the steps are falling. I don't want to get crippled.' Then Bill laughed.

On the back of the platform was a short bench, and Longley walked to this and sat down, calling for a drink of water. Someone handed him a dipperful and he drank it with relish, returned the cigar to his mouth, and resumed his inspection of the gallows.

Sheriff Brown immediately took charge of things, and, stepping forward to the front of the platform, addressed the crowd.

'This is the first legal hanging in Lee County, and I hope it will never be necessary to have another. Our object here is a solemn one and the duty a disagreeable one, but one that must be done.'

The sheriff's voice failed him as he searched in his pocket and drew out a folded paper. He rattled the paper nervously as he smoothed it out.

'At this time I must read the death warrant,' and this he proceeded to do, but before he had finished his voice was nothing more than a whisper.

Longley, still occupying his seat directly behind the swinging hemp, appeared the least concerned man in the entire crowd. As the sheriff concluded his reading, he motioned Longley to come forward.

'Speak now, Bill, say anything you want to say. It'll be your last chance.'

Longley patted the sheriff on the arm as if to encourage him against his blundering and took a step forward. Removing the cigar from his mouth, and in a clear voice which could be heard far back in the crowd, Bill spoke.

'I haven't much to say, but I hate to die surrounded by so many enemies and so few friends. I hope you will all forgive me for anything I have done. I have already forgiven all that did anything to me. God has forgiven me and I owe Him more than any of you. I know I have to die, and I hate it, for we all hate to die when the time comes, for I have killed many men who hated to die as bad as I do. If I have any friends about here who think of revenge, I hope they will forget it, as it is wrong. I hear my brother, Jim, is in the crowd. I hope not, but if he is I hope he will let revenge alone and pray for me, as I ask all others to do. I have taken enough revenge myself and must be punished for it. It is a debt I owe for my wild, reckless life. When it is paid, it will be over. I have nothing more to say.'

He put the cigar back in the corner of his mouth, then took it out quickly as a prayer was being offered by the priest.

Longley kissed Sheriff Brown and Father Spillard, then he put the black cigar back in his mouth, raised his manacled hands to the crowd, and in a strong, full voice shouted: 'Goodbye, all, goodbye!'

The black cap was drawn over Bill's head and the cigar fell

from under it to lay smoking on the pine planks at his feet. The ropes were adjusted, his arms and legs bound, and the word was given.

The trapdoor fell with a loud clatter and the body of Wild Bill Longley shot downward twelve feet, and came to a sudden jerk at the end of the rope. There was an iron rail underneath which held the trapdoor in place, and this swung against Bill's legs, knocking him sideways as he fell. As the body shot down, the rope slipped on the extended arm beam above the platform and the knees of Longley dragged the ground. Sheriff Brown and two deputies had to pull the body partly up again and hurriedly readjusted the rope. Eleven minutes later Doctors Johnson, Fields, and Gasley pronounced the gunman dead. After the body was cut down Sheriff Brown took Bill's head in his hands and turned it completely through 180 degrees. Brown placed the body in a covered hack, and the remains were taken to the cemetery and buried in a plain pine box on the outside of the iron fence.

There was nothing to mark the grave of Bill Longley except rude rocks which outlined it. Some twenty-five years later friends of the family erected over it a headstone made of a hollow petrified log.

Thus Lady Luck, who had been Longley's constant mistress for so many years, finally deserted him.

Or did she?

There were still the whispers. Still the unfounded stories and legends coming from just enough different places and people to make one wonder. Perhaps Longley had cheated the law and death so many times that no one believed he could die at the rope's end that afternoon in Giddings. Some said when the rope slipped and Bill's feet hit the ground his neck was not broken and he managed to stave off strangulation. Others said he had been fitted with a special harness which prevented any serious injury. As the stories go, Longley's 'dead body' eventually found its way to Central and South America. Where did these fantastic tales start?

In San Saba, Texas, several years ago a man who had been a close friend and neighbour to the Longleys told this story: Three days after the hanging his mother saw a covered wagon pull up to the back porch of the Longley ranch. The driver got out, untied the ropes at the back, and got in. A few minutes later two men got

63

out. Prior to that morning Longley's mother had been grief-stricken over her son's death. After the coming of the wagon she became more cheerful, almost happy, and went out of mourning. Was the second man Longley? And if so, how did he cheat the noose?

As late as 1892 Longley's father told an intimate friend that Bill was not hanged that day in Giddings. Old man Longley claimed that a rich uncle in California had put up forty thousand dollars to bribe the sheriff and doctors to rig the hanging so Longley could escape. A personal investigation shows that two of Bill's uncles did go to California prospecting for gold. One of them was injured in a mining accident; the other really struck it rich, retired from mining, built a fine hotel, refused to charge his friends, and didn't have any enemies, of course, under that arrangement, and soon went broke. It is believed that this uncle went broke *before* Bill was hanged.

In 1912 a young cousin of Bill then attending college in Russellville, Arkansas, was invited to the home of a fellow student. The student's father was a farmer of good standing in the community, with a fine wife and family. While there, the student's father told Longley's cousin a strange story. The farmer had once been a companion of Longley and had ridden with him on many occasions. They had parted company after the farmer killed a man in McLennan County, Texas, and fled to Arkansas to escape the law. There he had met and married a fine young woman, been converted to religion, and had confessed his crime. On the advice of his wife and pastor he had returned to Texas to stand trial and was acquitted.

'Is Bill Longley still alive?' the elderly man asked Bill's cousin.

'No, he was hanged in Giddings, Texas, many years before I was born,' came the reply.

'Yes, I know he was hanged, but he did not die. He may be alive today,' the farmer answered. Then he told Longley's cousin that he had received several letters from Longley, who had escaped to South America and was a rancher. At Longley's request he had burned the correspondence.

As late as 1934 an old gentleman, Captain John Talley, who knew both Longley and Wes Hardin, stated he did not believe Bill Longley was ever hanged. Mr. W. J. McClelland, who was one of Bill's guards, and who put the noose around Bill's neck, is absolutely positive that Longley died on the gallows in Giddings. As he termed it: 'Bill was deader'n a mackerel.'

Many people believe that had Longley escaped the hangman's knot that day he would eventually have come home to claim his dubious fame; that was like Bill. Some years ago a sexton at the cemetery where Bill's grave is located told of a visitor who came to the place—a tall grey-haired man who asked: 'Can you tell me where they say Bill Longley is buried?'

The sexton pointed to the piece of stone about two and a half feet high—the petrified wood—that stands at the head of the grave. The old man leaned on his cane, looked at the mound, then at the stone, and chuckling said: 'So that's where they say he's buried.' Then thanking the caretaker he turned and walked away. The old sexton to his dying day believed that Longley had come back to look at his own grave!

Oddly enough, when the *Lusitania* was torpedoed and sunk by the Germans on May 7, 1915, the passenger list of the doomed liner bore the name of W. P. Longley, South American cattleman!

The grave is still marked to this day. But what of the stories? Are they legend, like the legends that grew around so many of those Western figures, to cloud and distort the truth? Or did Longley's luck hold that grim morning in 1878 and help him cheat his executioners? Nobody ever bothered to open the grave when the stories began. Nobody checked. It would seem almost certain that Wild Bill did go to his just deserts that day in Giddings, but the doubts still prevail.

Only the grave knows the answer to the secret!

Colt's 1848 model, .44-calibre 6-shot

3 Cullen Baker

ALTHOUGH little has been written concerning the history of Cullen Baker, no doubt the shadow he cast across the great Republic of Texas eclipsed those cast by daring outlaws and gunmen who followed him. Baker's cunning nearly touched the sphere of insanity at times, and the best talents of the United States Army could not cope with him.

The son of a God-fearing young couple, Cullen Baker was born on June 22, 1835, in Weekly County, Tennessee.

In 1839 his father, John Baker, emigrated to the Red River country in Texas, arriving in Spanish Bluffs, Bowie County, late in December after a hardy trek in a small wagon with his family and their meagre possessions. The battle of San Jacinto had been fought and won by the Texans under Sam Houston only three years prior to that, and the only Government in Texas was in the hands of two rival gangs, who indulged regularly in murder and marauding. The territory of the new Republic of Texas was so great that it took a number of years to bring a semblance of law and order into being.

Perhaps in the hope of finding peace, John Baker moved his family forty miles away, to the south bank of the Sulphur Fork of the Red River, and began farming just west of the Arkansas state line. This region was in Cass County, which during the Civil War was renamed Davis County, in honour of the Confederate President Jefferson Davis.

As a ten-year-old boy Cullen was sallow-faced and slender, the butt of boys who were amused at his bare feet and homespun trousers. One day he sprang with fury upon the biggest of his tormentors and bested him. This first victory led him to dream of conquering imaginary monsters, and he spent a great deal of time wandering alone in the forest with a rifle, pretending to be stalking dangerous beasts. He practised continuously with the rifle as well as with an old six-gun he had managed to borrow. He became an expert marksman because he had plenty of time to practise throwing down with the rifle at a swift pace and drawing his revolver from his waistband with uncanny speed.

Because he liked to boast of his courage, it was a great disappointment to find himself without an opportunity for personal heroism. He made up for this by bragging of his aptness with the rifle and revolver; as a consequence, by the time he was sixteen every boy who knew him made a point of keeping out of his way. This, he told himself, was proof that he really was dangerous, and his bravado increased. In 1851 he started to drink whisky, and when he was 'high' he took pleasure in challenging any bystander to meet him in mortal combat. But his record as a crack shot was well known, and the townsfolk were careful not to give him any reason to draw his gun.

In his eighteenth year Cullen was still wearing homespun trousers with a single brace support held by pegs instead of buttons with a strap around his waist to hold his pistol. From under a slouch hat he squinted belligerently at anyone approaching him. He developed a quarrelsome disposition, and felt gratified when people backed away from him. On one occasion he displayed his menacing power before a crowd by forcing an old man to trot at the point of his gun. The sight of the old man's fear inspired him to continue the game beyond his original intention. He drove the old man out of town.

On another occasion Cullen gathered together some young men and started a battle against another group, all of them using knives and pistols, and the air rang with cries of mock-hatred. Cullen was felled by a blow from a tomahawk, and had to be kept in bed for several weeks.

During this period of suffering he seemed to look himself in the face, and it was confidently believed that he had reformed. Cullen told himself that the life of a gunfighter was not the thing; that some day another would come along and best him at his own game. In January 1854, while his head was still bandaged, he married Jane Petty, a seventeen-year-old who had faith in his good intentions. For nearly a year he lived like a respectable citizen, and people were inclined to think of his past mistakes as the wild oats sown by youth.

The era of the actual gunfighter had not yet arrived, and Cullen Baker had no challengers as yet to his claim of being one. Instead, he found glory in forcing men and boys to carry him on their shoulders through the streets, while he pecked them on the head with a knife or beat them with a pistol butt, to be sure they would obey his commands. Strangely enough, a large number of people succumbed to his bragging demands.

In August 1854 he used a leather whip to torment an orphan named Stallcup, and neighbours urged the boy to take the matter to court. At the trial a Mr. Baily, the well-respected head of a large family, testified against Cullen. He had been present during the beating. An hour after the trial Cullen appeared at Mr. Baily's home and yelled for him to come out. Baily stepped on to his porch, an old pistol in his hand.

'So you'd talk against me, eh, Baily?' sneered Baker. 'Well, you got a gun. Use it while you got the chance.'

Baily was no gunman, but he thought he might have a chance since his weapon already was in his hand. The pistol in Baily's hand bellowed and the slug whizzed past Baker's ear. Baily was in the process of trying a second shot when Baker's right hand snaked down and came up working his deadly pistol. The porch rocked with its roar, and blood spurted from the dumbfounded Baily's mouth as the first slug slammed him backward. The second bullet caught its victim smack in the forehead, and Mr. Baily fell dead.

Through the smoke haze the horrified family saw the father collapse. Mr. Baily's son, armed with his own rifle, tried to follow Cullen on foot, but Baker, being mounted, outdistanced him.

It was two years before young Baker was seen there again, and all members of his family, including his wife, had been without any news of him. When he reappeared in 1856 he learned that the authorities were still searching for him, and he left once more, for another two years. In 1858 he arranged to take his wife and baby

68

daughter to Perry County, Arkansas, where they made their home until Jane died on July 2, 1860.

Cullen carried the child back to the Sulphur country and left her with her grandfather, Hubbard Petty, who was living near Line Ferry. This apparently released him of all his parental and other responsibilities, and he made no further effort to discipline himself in any way.

Back in Perry County, while under the influence of alcohol, Baker got into a fight with a Mr. Wartham and killed him with a dagger.

The authorities made every effort to bring Baker to justice after this murder, but he eluded them and skipped out of Perry County, returning to Cass County in Texas, where he had been raised. Years had elapsed since his killing of Mr. Baily, and nobody was prepared to press the old charge against him. Cullen seemed to settle down. He made it clear that he wanted to become a new man.

As a result of this seeming reformation he won the love of Martha Foster, and they were married on July 1, 1862, apparently with the consent of her parents, William and Elizabeth Foster.

About this time he was conscripted into the Confederate Army and was ordered to Little Rock, Arkansas, with his company. He did not show any great loyalty to the service, but frequently went absent without leave to visit his wife. The gravity of the developing war situation must account for his officers' neglect in calling him to answer for these lapses.

While in the Army, Baker saw so much cruelty and death that his longing to become once more a gunfighter was revived. Again he slipped from his barracks and made his way to the Sulphur country. He decided to remain at home and raise corn for the troops. Since food was in constant demand throughout the war years, a farmer was considered to be doing patriotic work. Although Baker was a deserter, he thought he was doing the right thing.

Negroes seemed to have a special way of offending Baker for no explainable reason. In the spring of 1864 Baker was in Spanish Bluffs when a contingent of Negro troops under the command of Captain F. S. Dodge entered the town. These were Union soldiers looking for deserters from the Federal troops stationed in Missouri. Captain Dodge instructed the big sergeant to billet down at the end of town, but he had other ideas. The sergeant told the corporal to carry out the captain's orders while he and three Negro soldiers entered the one broken-down saloon the town boasted. At the bar stood a lone customer—Cullen Baker. The soldiers stopped short. It was not the vicious six-gun the man carried that stopped them, but the battered grey hat the stranger wore. It was Confederate issue!

But the sergeant's hesitation was only momentary.

'What's your name and where are you from?' he asked Baker.

Baker's hand darted down and came up filled with a blazing six-gun. The sergeant fell dead before he could raise a hand. The second bullet Baker fired killed a private as he darted for the door. The remaining pair died where they stood, their mouths gaping.

Cullen had killed the Union soldiers without thinking first. Now he was in trouble with both sides, but characteristically he left town hurriedly and joined the Federal troops at Little Rock. After he took the oath of allegiance he was placed in charge of a contingent of freedmen. But Baker still hated Negroes, and decided to return to the home of his uncle, Thomas Young. His uncle, afraid to cross Cullen, made him welcome.

One day Baker was out riding when some Jayhawkers overtook him and accused him of being a Federal. It took all his powers of persuasion to make them believe they were mistaken, and in a final effort to convince them he joined their ranks. In spite of their first suspicions and their constant watch over him, they soon discovered that he was their most talented member—for he showed great aptitude in handling weapons and got them out of several tight spots.

In October 1864 Baker heard that several citizens were trying to move out of the region which had been devastated by the Jayhawkers, so he waylaid them at the Saline River as they were embarking to cross.

'Hands up! Surrender!' Baker yelled.

'Who are you?' the emigrant leader retorted.

'We're outlaws and we want your goods.'

This incident caused Baker's promotion to leadership among the Freebooters, and after that he exercised his power upon every man who owned anything he wanted. His speed with the six-gun always convinced those who opposed him that he was no man to tangle with.

After one raid Baker found they were being closely pursued by a strong posse, so they abandoned their loot and scattered wildly. Baker with three of his companions rode into Davis County, where he had been raised, but when news of his new activities arrived he left suddenly. He attempted to enlist some new followers for another bandit company, but did not succeed until February 1865.

In the meantime Baker's wife was still living with her father near Line Ferry. She heard a rumour that her husband had been captured at Little Rock and was being court-martialled. Fearing that he would be sentenced to death, and desperately wanting to be with him until the last, she deceived her family by pretending to visit a nearby neighbour. Then through a violent winter storm, without adequate clothing and with no supplies, she rode two hundred miles. When she discovered that the rumour was mistaken, and that her husband was merely in the hills organizing a new command for himself, she rode another thirty-six hours through a snowstorm to the home of Thomas Young, hoping that this uncle would have news of her husband.

Indeed, Baker did visit his uncle while his wife was there, and he was angry that she had followed him.

He said: 'I wish you had been sick enough so as not to be able to move a hand or foot, so then you would have stayed home where you belong.'

But she remained in the household of Mr. Young until the spring. Then, after Baker had made a number of raids upon scouting parties and Army posts, he took his wife back over the two hundred miles to their home in the Sulphur country. The Army of the Trans-Mississippi Department had now surrendered, and the war was reaching its end.

In July Baker met some of his former cronies on their way back to Davis County, and he congratulated them on the number of cattle and horses they had commandeered. While they were riding together he made a stop at the farm of Mrs. Drew, near Jefferson. Tearfully she told him of the raid on her ranch, and Baker made a great show of being horrified at this outrage perpetrated upon her. He even offered to try to get her cattle back. In gratitude Mrs. Drew offered a reward if he was successful.

Baker rode away, caught up with his companions, and selected Mrs. Drew's cattle from their haul. Then he returned the beasts to

Mrs. Drew and accepted the bonus as well as her heartfelt thanks. In fact, Mrs. Drew gave this deed of Baker's such wide publicity that many people began to doubt he could be the unscrupulous individual they had heard he was.

Late that autumn Baker thought of settling down at Musk Island, ten miles north of Line Ferry, and starting a competing ferry as his own enterprise. But he was taken sick and had to abandon that project. He and his wife continued to live with her parents, the Fosters, until January 10, 1866. On that date they moved to Line Ferry, and Baker began to operate the boat from there.

On March 1 his wife died, and he seems to have been truly grief-stricken. At any rate, he made an effigy of her in clothes which she had worn, and he kept it standing in a life-like pose for all the neighbours to see. It was several weeks before he was prevailed upon to remove it.

But two months after his wife's burial he called on the Fosters again and proposed marriage to his sister-in-law, Bell, who was then sixteen. This proposal was declined by both Bell and her parents. Baker left them with a new bitterness in his heart.

Probably he sensed that the young school-teacher, Thomas Orr, who was boarding with the Fosters at the time, had won the fancy of young Bell. Earlier, in January, Baker had been one of the sponsors of this school-teacher, and had shown him considerable friendship. But on June 2, a month after Bell had refused to marry him, Baker forced a fight upon Orr.

Orr was just crossing the ferry during Baker's temporary absence at the grocer's. Baker reached the north bank with a jug of whisky, and waited until the boat landed. He insisted that Orr drink with him. When Orr explained that he never touched alcohol, Baker took personal affront and started a fight.

Not only was Orr a studious man and far from muscular, but his right hand was deformed from rheumatism. Naturally Baker was getting the best of the fight, as John Herring, the operator of the boat during Baker's absence, later explained, for he stood by during the fracas, not daring to interfere. Baker made short work of the battle by hitting Orr on the head with a pine bough. When Orr fell to the ground Baker jumped into the boat and rowed off.

Orr was bleeding copiously when he regained consciousness. Herring helped him to mount the little roan which belonged to Mr. Foster. It was the same horse that Baker's wife had ridden on her wild ride through the storm to see her husband before his supposed execution. As quickly as he could, Orr rode to the home of Dr. Oats and had his wounds dressed. Until that day he had never suspected this violent side of Baker's character. In January he had arrived as a stranger. He could only explain Baker's violence by saying: 'No doubt the whisky went to Cullen's head.'

However, when he was told of Baker's past wild life and his swiftness with the revolver, he expressed surprise that the authorities should countenance such actions. He procured a pistol and meant to have it out with Baker on his return trip. But friends persuaded him to go home by a different route.

It was a month later when Baker arrived at the schoolhouse while Orr was teaching and angrily demanded the ferry fare which Orr had forgotten to pay in the excitement of the fight. Orr paid it readily. Then, right before the class, Baker treated the school-teacher to a tirade of abusive language.

'I'll shoot your head off smooth with your shoulders if I hear you telling any lies about me,' Baker threatened.

After this scene one of the pupils, George Couch, walked out of the schoolhouse and attached himself to Baker as an enthusiastic admirer. Later George Couch delivered a letter to the school-teacher:

> *Line Ferry, Arkansas*
> July 20, 1866
>
> THOAS ORR SIR If you wish to Teach your School you had bitter bea at it every day I here of you Beeing fishing. My Lad you Don't No that my Gizzard is Grinding on Dam lies that you told over the River Don't let me here of you beaing absent from that School Any more fir It is all that I Can do to keep from giving you another & good call & if I find one thing to Bee so You may Look for me I am Sir yours as Mad as Hell till Death.
>
> CULLEN M. BAKER

Thoas Orr at Home I don't Want the friendship Any one that you Can turn Against me.

Govner Orr at Home.

Though the missive has been described as an example of handsome penmanship, it can hardly be claimed that it is couched in the language of the scholar some people later pretended Cullen Baker had been.

After delivery of the letter some civic-minded residents of the region consulted the Justice of the Peace, but were informed that nothing could be done to stop Baker's progress farther into crime. It was evident that everyone was afraid of that swift gun hand of his. The patrons of the school held a mass meeting and discussed the possibility of capturing Baker in order to put a stop to his career, but one elderly gentleman urged them to take a more humane step towards correcting the difficulty. This member of the meeting suggested sending a delegation to deal with the outlaw, and, as it later turned out, he himself was the first member of that particular crowd to be killed by Baker. He was William Foster, not to be confused, however, with Baker's father-in-law of the same name.

The delegation did wait on Baker, intimating that the populace wanted to know his intentions for the future, and Baker made some heavy threats about what he would do if anybody attempted to interfere with his freedom. Nevertheless, he was finally prevailed upon to offer this much of an appeasement:

Line Ferry, Arkansas
July 27, 1866.

I hereby sertify to the Neighbors of Hiett's Bind that I will in No Manner Interrupt Nor Bother one Thos Orr further more I Consider my word as good as any Body's or as good as the word of Jesus Christ J witness my hand.

C. M. BAKER

Two days later Baker wrote another letter and had it delivered to his father-in-law by Samuel Couch:

Line Ferry, Arkansas
July 29, 1866

MR. FOSTER Dear Sir Dear Father as I should say for you have bin a father to me So has Mrs. Foster Bin a Mother but I Recken you Both have Resind to Bee any more therefore I think It In vain to Ever Look for Either of you here any more and Whereas I have Bin Requested to Inform you of a Matter Concerning some Pills that the Old Man Bevel Requested you to take In Charge some years ago that he had left with some one Near Bright Star he Wanted you to send the Money for them here to me So he Could get it or Leave Word What you Done about them as he will be here Soon again.

Mr. Foster It is very hard for me to Bear and how it is that One Can throw away an old friend for a New one Mrs. Foster has surely here tofore held Me as a friend But she is now laboring under a wide mistake or Wanting me to put that that Dont fit me and wear It In Behald of that Damd Orr She Cannot think that I am mistake in a matter of that kind that has such an impression on my Mind as that Did If I had Killed Jesus Christ It would not Raised half the excitement this matter has I hope and Pray to live the ten months out and keep my Same mind for I am not a Negro Neither am I bound In this country I No that I am a Liar and a Drunkard and a Devil But I never tell lies on my Friends.

The matter Raised Between us the other Day has give me no Little Trouble But as I sayd In a Note to Orr I dont want the friendship of any One that he In any manner Can turn against Me I commenced in trouble and End in the same Hoping to see the 15th day of December.

C. M. BAKER

Wm. Foster Hyettes Bend, Arks

The date, December 15, is mentioned in this letter because Baker assumed that the school would close on that date and that Thomas Orr would probably thereupon leave that locality. However, the school closed on November 2, ten scholastic months after January 28, when Orr had first begun his duties.

Of course when November 2 arrived Baker knew very well that the school was closed. On November 3 he went to the home of the Fosters, hoping that Orr had left—perhaps even hoping that, in the absence of Orr, Bell Foster might look more favourably upon himself. Out of bravado he rode up to the house surrounded by five large mastiffs and searched the premises for Orr. After a while he blew a horn to call off the dogs and rode away. Doubtless he thought he was cutting a heroic figure for Bell's benefit.

It is true that Orr had left immediately after closing the school the previous day. But on hearing about Baker's dramatic circling of the Fosters' home, he tried to file a complaint with the Justice of the Peace and the County Sheriff. They both assured him they could do nothing in the matter. He then decided to waylay Baker on

75

December 30 at Day's Creek, and there he waited most of the afternoon. But when some of Baker's associates passed by he supposed they would warn him, so he gave up the idea and went home. Nevertheless, Baker had not been advised of Orr's presence at Day's Creek, and about fifteen minutes after Orr gave up he crossed the bridge on his way to spend the night at the home of a Mr. Mayes.

Baker fancied himself as courting Mr. Mayes's daughter, and he told her she might expect him to pay another call on Wednesday evening. This promise reached Orr, who himself arrived on Wednesday evening. But Baker in the meantime had returned to Line Ferry.

When he was unable to outbid others for the Line Ferry concession, Baker threatened to run it anyhow. He went to Linden, Texas, to procure a licence, defying any man to compete with him, and emphasizing that his fast gun would back him up. But he gave up this plan shortly and instead chose a spot seven miles beyond the Texas state line, where he started a ferry of his own.

Orr, eager to avoid any further meeting with the desperado, took another school three miles farther into the State of Arkansas, hoping that there he would be left in peace. However, he continued to keep a double-barrelled gun and a six-shooter handy.

Baker now became so embittered that he turned his spite on anyone whom he thought had insulted him. He also continued to send threatening notes to Thomas Orr, who believed that there must be some misunderstanding to have caused this rupture between them. He made one more effort to heal the breach. On April 27, 1867, he wrote:

MR. CULLEN BAKER, Sir: I have written to you before but have not received any answer. It may be possible that you did not receive the note. I, therefore, embrace the present opportunity of writing again. I suppose, or at least have heard, that you say you have nothing against me. I would be glad to know that it was a fact. I have also heard that you said you had understood that I had threatened your life. As to your having heard it, of course, I cannot deny, as I am not accountable for lies told by others. All that I can ask is for a man to be produced who ever heard me make any such assertion.

It would be a great pleasure to me if our difficulty could be settled, and we were, or could become, as we once were. If I had, or could be convinced, that I have any acknowledgments to make, I would do it with pleasure; but I don't consider that I ever gave you any reason for treating me as you have, and I am not aware of giving you any cause for even being mad at me; besides, I am not appraised of what you got mad about. I want to go over the river occasionally and I have been compelled to put myself to much trouble and inconvenience, and have been deprived of the pleasures and comforts of life to keep out of your presence, and to prevent the execution of what I have feared to be your intentions. I hope to hear from you soon.

Yours respectfully,
THOMAS ORR

This civilized gesture meant nothing to Baker, for his hatred of his rival for Bell Foster's attentions continued to make him want to plot revenge. Orr had no realization that this was the root of the trouble between him and Baker.

About June 1 Baker went to Rowden's grocer's store on the road between Jefferson and Line Ferry and found it closed and the storekeeper absent. He demanded the keys from Mrs. Rowden and entered the store and took what he wanted. When Mr. Rowden heard of this, he went to call on Baker and asked for payment. He also took along a shotgun loaded with slugs.

'Oh, sure,' said Baker. 'I'll pay you in a few days.'

Some nights later Baker appeared at the Rowden gate, shouting for Mr. Rowden to come down at once. Recognizing Baker's voice, Mrs. Rowden and her daughter begged Mr. Rowden not to reply, but Mr. Rowden saw no reason to be alarmed. He picked up his shotgun and stepped out.

'What do you mean by speaking disrespectfully to me?' Baker demanded.

'I'm sure I never meant to do such a thing,' Mr. Rowden began.

He never had a chance to use the scattergun, for like a striking rattlesnake Baker's six-gun snapped up. Four times it barked, and four slugs slammed into Rowden's body. Hurled forward, dead on his feet, he pitched headlong to the ground,

When he heard that citizens were organizing in order to capture him, Baker issued a proclamation that he would gun down any man who dared to accuse him of killing Mr. Rowden except in a fair fight. The Federal commander at Jefferson, Texas, now sent a squad with instructions to bring Baker in, but before they could surround him he had left the state again.

As a matter of fact, he returned within a few days well armed and rode about the district, loudly defying the Federal authorities. But mostly he stayed in the byways of Sulphur Bottom, where he had camped during the latter part of the Civil War while avoiding the conscript agents. Now he made his home among the pines and oaks or in the swamps. Gradually he became bolder, helped himself to the best horseflesh he could find, and kept himself in ammunition by daring forages.

The troops were still supposed to be scouting for him, but nobody dared to give information about his whereabouts. Unlike Jesse and Frank James and the Youngers, who were to follow, he remained immune because people were afraid to talk. In the case of the Jameses and the Youngers, folks were proud to hide them.

After scouting in Bowie County Baker turned to Davis County. At Pett's Ferry, on the Sulphur, he was overtaken by the advance guard of a company trying to locate him. He had just crossed the river on the ferry when the guard rode up and engaged him in conversation.

'What's your name?' asked the sergeant.

'It's Johnson,' lied Baker, 'but what in hell makes you so particular?'

'We thought you might be Cullen Baker, the man we are searching for,' replied the sergeant. 'From your arms and the way you're dressed I'm inclined to believe you are Baker.'

As the sergeant started to draw his revolver Baker's hand snapped up, and his own revolver belched flame. Three bullets spun the soldier from his saddle, and he was dead before he struck the ground. The frightened private who accompanied the ill-fated sergeant raced his mount back to warn the detachment.

Baker pushed deeper into the swamp and wound along the southern bank of the Sulphur for several miles. At a shallow place which was well known to him he forded the river, returning to Bowie County. The troops also crossed the river again and rode towards Boston, not realizing that they were drawing near to their quarry.

Baker heard them approaching his hiding-place and, indeed,

78

watched them as they drew nearer. At a crossroads he shouted from the bushes in a loud command: 'Charge them, boys! Charge them!'

Evidently the troops believed that the woods were full of Baker's men, for they galloped off in panic. Coming out of hiding, Baker picked up an officer's hat which had fallen during the hasty retreat.

At another time when he felt particularly daring Baker exposed himself before a score of well-disciplined soldiers. They immediately fired on him. He discharged both barrels of his shotgun before resorting to his fast-firing six-shooters. The Federals were driven away in disorder, leaving one of their comrades on the ground dead. Though Baker was wounded in the right arm, he was able to mount his mule and ride off. The pain made it necessary for him to stop after covering two miles, but he was not followed.

The Federal officers were determined to get him, and they dispatched a courier for reinforcements. As soon as they had enough soldiers, they spread throughout the region on the lookout. But there were still a number of Southern sympathizers who considered Baker a Yankee-killer, and refused to help the Federals round him up. His fame as a dare-devil spread, and fresh troops were ordered to Eastern Texas from every state in the Union with the express command to get Cullen Baker. Still he reconnoitred through the familiar swamps and dense forests of Sulphur, keeping comfortably hidden unless he needed provender for his mount. He helped himself to whatever he wanted, the farmers always remaining carefully out of sight when he appeared. After a few weeks the Federals reported the chase fruitless and returned to Jefferson.

On October 10 Baker was riding along the road between Linden and Boston when he passed a Government wagon without thinking much about it. However, on reflection he decided to capture its cargo. He turned his horse and rode past it again, getting far enough ahead to be able to secrete himself in the bushes. When the wagon approached he stepped into the road and ordered the driver to halt. The driver made a heroic effort to draw his Service revolver, but Baker killed him before the gun had cleared leather. The four soldiers who were supposed to guard the supplies fired on Baker and then fled, leaving him in possession of the stores. He carried the stock into Sulphur Bottom and stacked it away for future use.

When the guard returned to Jefferson with the news of this latest attack a large force was sent in pursuit, but returned unsuccessful. The military commander then offered a reward of a thousand dollars for the capture of Cullen Baker.

During that autumn Baker remained in Arkansas unmolested. On Christmas Day he bought several gallons of whisky at Bright Star and invited a group of men to drink as much as they wanted. After they had become intoxicated he led them to Howell Smith's farm in Sulphur, arriving after dark. Looking through the windows, he saw several freedmen sitting about the fire, where they were waiting for their own quarters to be prepared for them. Baker and his jolly colleagues fired through the windows, and in the mêlée one of his own men shot him in the right thigh.

The shooting over, Baker found himself deserted as he lay on the ground wounded. Even his horse had been taken by one of his boon companions. Though he found a mule, he was not strong enough to mount. But he saw Mr. Smith's two daughters in the dark, and he ordered them to assist him in mounting the mule.

He rode to Mr. Foster's house, about a mile away, and urged Mr. Foster to see if the Smiths needed assistance.

A courier was dispatched to Jefferson, Texas, where Captains Scott and Allen raised a volunteer company of citizens to go in pursuit of Baker. But the culprit remained safely at Mr. Foster's house for about sixty hours before he returned to the woods. General McGloffin arrived with his command of regulars to join the volunteers. Both the troops and the citizens met at Mr. Smith's house late in the afternoon to discuss tactics. They felt there was no use doing anything until the following morning.

Of course, by the time they found signs of Baker's night camp he had evacuated to a safer place. Though scouts trailed him into the Sulphur bottomlands, the main contingent was delayed by its very size. But they hurried on.

When the advance patrol caught sight of Baker's new camp they shouted the alert to the entire command. The troops and citizens all rushed forward, firing from every direction. At the first sound of the attack Baker calmly mounted a horse he had ready saddled for such an emergency, and became lost in the dense forest.

By January 1, 1868, more than three hundred men, both soldiers and civilians, were travelling under arms in search of the gunman-desperado, while twice that number remained at home well armed in case he should appear unexpectedly. But no trace of Baker was found again until the following October, when he appeared in Boston, Texas. There he walked boldly up to Captain Kirkham, the bureau agent, and said: 'I'm Cullen Baker. You looking for me?'

The astonished agent made a frantic effort to grab a nearby pistol, but to no avail. Baker's six-gun leaped up and spit fire, sending a lethal slug into the captain's head. Governor Clayton then posted a reward of a thousand dollars for the outlaw's arrest.

By November 1 Baker had accumulated a score of followers, and with them he crossed Red River and raided several farms in Sevier and Little River Counties, Arkansas. In this foray two Government officers, Andrews and Willis, were killed.

Governor Clayton now called out the State Militia under the command of General Catterson. Warned of this, Baker crossed the Red River and called at Dr. Jones's farm, explaining that he was a Militia officer in search of Cullen Baker. The farmer gave him supplies, and for a time was none the wiser that he had outfitted the dreaded fugitive.

Later Baker took his small force to the home of James Salmon shortly before daylight, calling Mr. Salmon to come down, since the Federals wanted to talk with him. As soon as the door opened, the outlaw rushed in, seized Salmon and tied a rope around his neck and secured his hands behind his back. Then his men plundered the house.

It was already daylight when Baker and his gang arrived at the home of Mr. Scarborough. They called him to come out, but Mr. Scarborough refused to surrender until Baker had assured him for a third time that he would not be harmed. Later Baker persuaded Mr. Scarborough to promise that he would talk to Captain Scott and others to inquire if a compromise could be arranged.

From there Baker led his men to Parson Jesse Dobbs's house and held him captive all day until he, too, agreed to try to effect a compromise.

Scarborough and Dobbs did make the attempt, and a meeting of citizens finally came to the conclusion that a compromise was the best they could effect. A day was designated for a meeting at which all people interested should forgather at Scott's Mill, Davis County, Texas. Baker offered to give a bond in the amount of two hundred

Great Gunfighters of the West

thousand dollars on his good behaviour from then on, with the best security Bowie County could afford. Everybody seemed to consider this good news, and plans were made for the general amnesty.

Baker did not appear, however. And even while the compromise was being discussed at the mass meeting Baker shot and killed another Federal soldier in a duel.

The next move made by the citizenry was to send a committee to meet Baker and inquire his intentions. As a result of the good offices of three citizens, R. P. Crump, F. M. Henry, and R. M. Stewart, he permitted a friend to write the following letter, which appeared in the *Weekly Austin Republican* under the date of December 2, 1868, as well as in the *Jefferson Times* and the *Jimplecute*:

Bowie County, Texas
November 14, 1868

Editors of the *Times*:

Permit me to publish a statement in your paper in order to place myself right before the Government and the people of the country. Various rumours have obtained circulation through the country in regard to my course of conduct; and many persons are now committing offences against law and good order, on my credit. And hence, I deem it necessary to declare my sentiments and intentions for the future. It is rumoured that I have said that no civil officers should perform the duties of their offices in the counties where I stay. To which report I have to say, that I am strictly in favour of the enforcement of the civil laws of the country by the legitimate authorities. And I now declare that it shall be my steady purpose to *protect the quiet* citizen and his labourers, either white or black, in the pursuit of their avocations. And I request all good citizens to *inform me* of all depredations committed by other persons, charged to have been committed by me. This is my native country, and my interests are identical with those of other citizens of the country; and I hope to remain in the counties of Davis, Bowie, Marion and the adjoining counties in Eastern Texas. And I further declare, that it will not be *my purpose to make war* upon the good and peaceable citizens or labourers of this or any other section. Nor do I intend to interfere in any way with the powers that be. The white man and the black man will be perfectly safe in my hands so long as he lets me alone and pursues his peaceful and lawful business.

By accident, I happened to detect a party of five men on Col. Hook's farm, on Red River, robbing and plundering the Negroes, taking from them guns, ammunition, needles, soap, and every other small article of value, calling themselves Cul Baker, Bickerstaff and company. I arrested the parties, and found their names to be J. Sharp, J. Poterfield, George Robertson, George Franks and Tom Franks—all of whom I denounce as being beneath contempt. I disarmed said party, relieved them of their plunder, which I returned to the proper owners, and sent the scoundrels to their homes. I would have carried them to Boston and had them committed to jail by the civil authorities, but heard there were no officers in the county in whose charge I could place them. When the said parties were discharged I notified them that if I ever caught them under like circumstances, they would not again be dealt with. In conclusion, I have to say that I am not the great manslayer that scandal has made me—killing white and black wherever found, and I am determined in the future to do all the good I can for the peaceable and quiet citizens in the country where I stay. I shall in future publish the causes that led me into my present difficulties, and feel satisfied that I shall not be deemed by a just community, wholly to blame for my action in the past. I am now, and have ever been, willing to submit the whole of my conduct to a decision of unbiased men of my country, and abide by their just verdict.

Your obedient servant,

CULLEN M. BAKER

Whoever acted as Baker's ghost-writer on this occasion was adept at making an impression of power and virtue. Certainly Baker believed himself to be able to control other plunderers and to be willing to champion the innocent, for his whole view was distorted in his own benefit.

The citizens who had effected this much of an agreement were required to back it up, undoubtedly under duress, and they appended these words to the above letter:

Jefferson,
November 16, 1868

We, the undersigned, have to state that at the request of a number of citizens of Davis County, we went out in search of Cullen M. Baker, to see him and ascertain from him what his course in the future would be. We found him, and the result of the interview with him, was as above set forth in his card, which we believe he will abide by.

R. P. CRUMP
F. M. HENRY
R. M. STEWART

The Weekly Austin Republican made a sarcastic comment:

So Cullen M. Baker has assumed the protection of quiet citizens. As the chicks shelter under the wings of the parent bird, so may all apprehensive souls rest under the aegis of this thief and murderer! Let all good citizens report to him; he will see their wrongs righted. They, black and white, will be 'safe' in his hands! And R. P. Crump, F. M. Henry, and R. M. Stewart go bail for him!—We miss the name of W. P. Saufley on the back of this paper. It naturally belongs there; and for the want of it we send the document to the nearest notary for protest.

Seldom have we seen a more melancholy instance of moral perversion than this manifesto. Long success in outrage has so inflamed the vanity of Cullen M. Baker that he imagines himself a power in the State, and condescends to be gracious.

. . . We cannot imagine what Messrs. Crump and Co. think of Cullen M. Baker or of themselves. Other honest men 'in search of' him, if as fortunate as they were in finding him, would have bound him hand and foot, and would have left him at the nearest military post to answer for his manifold atrocities. But they, after a cordial interview with this outlawed felon, return by themselves and endorse his word of honour!

Thomas Orr had by this time been married to Bell Foster for about a year. He was teaching school in Lafayette County, eight miles north-west of Line Ferry. But he and his wife were spending the winter at Mr. Foster's house four miles south-east of Line Ferry. He and Baker had not met for more than two years. Naturally Orr had no confidence in Baker's promise to kill no more, and he still went armed.

On November 20 Baker had accumulated a small army on the grounds that he wanted to cross the Red River in pursuit of the Militia, in order to recapture property they had unjustly confiscated and to redress wrongs inflicted by them upon various citizens. He paraded all the men he could muster and started a march towards Little Rock, enlisting recruits as he went. But when he had gathered together as many young men as believed his claims, he recrossed Red River, explaining that he had to go into Lafayette, Bowie, and Davis Counties to meet the balance of his contingent.

The Militia had set out for Little Rock to meet him, but after hearing of his raid into Sevier County they faced about and proceeded to Red River.

On December 7 Baker and his men appeared before Mr. Foster's home. It was then ten o'clock and the family had gone to bed. The outlaws surrounded the house and demanded Mr. Foster come forth.

Mr. Foster went to the door and with some dignity demanded: 'What is the cause of this untimely visit?' taking it for granted that his long years of kindness to this former son-in-law entitled him to courtesy.

'We want Thomas Orr,' cried Baker, giving way once again to his long-dissembled purpose to punish the man who had won Bell's love.

Orr agreed to surrender after Baker assured him that he would not be harmed, for this seemed to be the only way he could save his young wife from molestation. Baker kept the prisoner under close watch all night, glorying in this opportunity to prove to Bell that he was master of her husband.

About sun-up the whole band started off in a westerly direction, Thomas Orr being forced to ride behind a boy, still tied, while Baker held one end of the rope about Orr's neck as they rode. Half a mile off Baker tied his end of the rope to a dogwood branch and commanded the boy to ride his horse forward. That left Orr suspended by the neck, his feet dangling in air.

Later when Baker needed rope with which to hang another victim, he cried: 'Cut down that wretch and drag him away! And bring me that rope.'

When the marauders rode off to Bright Star for a fresh supply of whisky, they left Orr lying on the frozen ground.

The following day Baker rode on his way to Rondo. At Rondo two companies of citizens had organized under orders from General Catterson. Several thousand troops had also been ordered to capture the desperado. Baker himself had only a score of followers.

On December 10 Baker crossed into Texas, going westward as far as Mount Pleasant. On December 20 he returned to Davis County and was very nearly captured before he retreated across the Sulphur. About January 1, 1869, the Federal troops once again abandoned the chase and returned to Jefferson.

On January 4 Baker recrossed the Sulphur at Musk Island, and the next day returned to the place where he had killed Mr. Baily.

He took Mr. Haynes into custody and held him in his camp over-night.

'What do you know about Thomas Orr?' Baker asked him.

'I suppose he's dead,' said Mr. Haynes. 'I heard that you hung him about a month ago.'

'I hung him, but he's not dead,' said Baker. 'I have heard from him since. But one of us has got to die, and that before long.'

'I guess you mean before tomorrow's setting sun,' said Mr. Haynes grimly.

On January 6 Baker started for Arkansas, a two-and-a-half-hour ride. After crossing the state line he and his companion proceeded directly to Mr. Foster's house.

Thomas Orr was in the house and saw them approaching, but when they passed by he concluded that they must be on their way to Mr. Lamar's place, where several men had assembled to butcher hogs. He slipped out, and by a circuitous route through the woods reached that place. He found Baker had already been there.

Thomas Orr called upon the men at Lamar's to help him track down and kill Baker. Only three of the men offered to go with him.

A mile away Baker had stopped for a bite of lunch, thinking he was perfectly safe. His pursuers came quickly and discharged half a dozen guns at him, killing him and his companion instantly. It would have been suicide for Orr to try capturing Baker or to call him into a fair fight. A direct attack was what he thought best. Indeed, it was the only way for a novice gunman like him. Future outlaws and gunmen met the same fate—a bullet in the back: Jesse James, Wild Bill Hickok, John Wesley Hardin, Ben Thompson, and King Fisher, to mention but a few.

The attackers found on Baker's corpse a double-barrelled shot-gun, four six-shooters, three derringers, several silver dollars, twenty-seven assorted keys, six pocket-knives. He had also been carrying a copy of the *Louisville Courier Journal* of December 16, 1868. In vanity Baker had marked this item:

Cullen Montgomery Baker, the Arkansas brigand, and his band, have left the State to join the Cuban expedition. If Clayton's militia could be induced to go to Cuba, Halifax or any place else, the State would enjoy peace and prosperity.

In spite of the years through which many official attempts had been made to capture Cullen M. Baker, it was the studious school-teacher with the withered right hand who finally closed his notorious career.

Those with a penchant for painting vicious, swaggering gunmen and usually neurotic killers as frontier Robin Hoods have not overlooked Cullen Baker, although very little research has been done on him in the past. The few who have written about him have shown him as a brave, soft-spoken, courteous Southerner ever respectful to women, a man of high ethics, who was forced to live by the gun. And in all fairness, Baker did have guts . . . but there his virtue ended.

.45-calibre Colt's Peacemaker (1873)

4 Bat Masterson

WILLIAM BARCLAY MASTERSON, far better known as Bat Masterson, whose life has been so authentically portrayed and publicized by Gene Barry on the television screen, was born on a farm in Iroquois County, Illinois. He was the second of Thomas and Catherine Masterson's six children. The parents met and married in upstate New York, began raising a family in Illinois, moved to Missouri shortly after the Civil War, and later migrated to Kansas, where they settled on a prairie homestead eighteen miles north of Wichita.

Bat had two sisters, Minnie and Nellie, and three brothers, Ed, Jim, and Tom. Ed was the oldest and most cherished, not only by Bat but all the others, particularly his mother. In most large families there seems to be one member with a noticeable grace and gentleness. Among the Mastersons this paragon was Ed, the peacemaker, the pale dreamer, who always seemed a little too good for the rough world into which he had been born. According to the rules of psychology, Bat and Ed should have been rivals and enemies, especially since Mrs. Masterson never made any secret of her preference for Ed, but it was simply impossible to hate or envy the older boy. Instead of being possessed by a Cain-like hatred, Bat felt protective towards his older brother, an attitude that was to endure into manhood, until the tragic evening when even that staunch loyalty was not sufficient.

Bat was Ed's opposite, lively, aggressive, full of pranks, always in trouble, or on the edge of trouble, or looking for trouble. He was the eternal Huck Finn, and the scant education provided for families in the sod huts of the Kansas homesteaders did not dismay him in the least. Self-education and a resourceful mind later supplied much that should have been instilled by a prairie schoolmarm, but spelling always remained something of a mystery to him. This weakness was illustrated by a letter he wrote to the Colt firearm factory at the age of thirty-one, beginning: 'Gents, Please send me one of your nickle-plated .45 calibor revolvers. It is for my own use and for that reason I would like to have a little extra paines with it . . .'

The sort of education that Bat wanted was not to be found in any classroom. It was provided eventually by a pre-Civil War musket acquired by his father in a swapping session with a townsman. The elder Masterson proposed to trade it off for something more useful on the farm, but Bat persuaded his father to keep it. The gun wasn't worth much. It was an old Springfield that had probably seen service in the Mexican War, and was jerked from its rack in the St. Louis arsenal to help arm one of the amateur regiments that saved the Border States for the Union during the early years of the Civil War.

But it meant a lot to Bat. A boy growing up on the frontier considered himself practically naked without a firearm of some kind. His powers of persuasion must have been considerable even then, in his early teens. He took the smoothbore musket to a blacksmith with whom he had struck up a warm friendship, and talked the old fellow into rifling the barrel of his gun so that it would shoot farther and straighter. Bat became a crack shot, practising behind the barn with the old musket.

Another essential of his education was provided by occasional trips in the spring wagon to Wichita. That dusty trail-town was a place of evil splendour to Bat, with its saloons, gambling houses, dance-halls, variety theatres, horse traders' corrals, stores, and hotels, ramshackle as this cowtown would have appeared to the infrequent visitor from the East.

Even more fascinating were the men who swaggered along its streets, all of them with a great pride of occupation. You could tell at a glance what a man did for a living—the tall-hatted Texas cowpunchers, the merchants with their boiled shirts and string ties, the scrofulous and blood-smeared buffalo hunters, the gamblers immaculate in broadcloth and silk hats. Of the whole passing scene, the boy gaping from his perch on the hitching-rack was especially fascinated by the gamblers. They exuded such a worldly air with their pomaded hair, carefully tended moustaches, diamond rings and heavy gold watch-chains, and their measured geniality. But his eyes bugged out even more at the men he heard talked about only in whispers—the gunfighters. Quiet, self-contained men to whom others gave respectful berth along the crowded boardwalks. Lonely men set apart from their fellows by their godlike tendency to dispatch lesser men to another world. And there were the females. They came in two classes, as Bat knew, good and bad. There were the bedizened women of the town, the girls who worked in dance-halls, the actresses who played in the variety theatres, and there were women like his mother and sisters. But all these people represented the adventure he knew he would never find following the plough on his father's farm.

He was seventeen when he managed to persuade Ed, who was a year older, that it was time for them to venture forth on their own. Ed agreed that the farm did not produce enough as yet to keep them all in abundance, and that the younger brothers were hefty enough to help their father. The two brothers decided to head for Western Kansas, which was enjoying a boom in the buffalo-hide market.

The first place they stopped was Dodge City, the wildest town on the frontier. The Atchison, Topeka, and Santa Fe Railroad was then stretching west through Kansas towards Colorado.

The rail company provided Bat and Ed with their first jobs. They obtained a subcontract from a contractor named Ritter to grade the right of way a mile west from Fort Dodge. It was along that stretch that Front Street sprang up in all its crapulous glory.

When they finished the back-breaking job they found that Mr. Ritter, taking advantage of their innocence, had skipped out and neglected to pay them the three hundred dollars promised for the grading. Heart-broken and purse-broken, they considered their next move.

'I think I'll go home and see Ma and the kids,' Ed said. 'I've been mighty homesick, Billy, and I can't hide it any more. You better come with me, as it's better than starving and being cheated out here.'

'I'll be damned if I will!' Bat said. 'I'm going to stay here and lay for Ritter. He owes us three hundred dollars and he's going to pay up or I'll put a slug in him. I'll just wait here for a while, Ed. Ritter's going to be passing through here one of these days. The railroad will be pushing on for Granada across the Colorado line, and he's got contracts to fill up ahead.'

So Ed went home and Bat went to work driving a team for a local tycoon named Tom Nixon, no longer an independent sub-contractor, but a mere hireling like the swarm of Orientals and Irish working on the railtracks. Not long afterwards, however, a friend came to Bat with the news that Ritter was 'coming through on tomorrow's train and has a roll of three thousand dollars on his hip'.

Bat, who had bought a six-shooter with his wages as a teamster, was waiting when the westbound train rolled in the next day. He boarded it and found Ritter sitting in one of the cars. He forced his debtor out on the platform at gunpoint. A crowd of loafers had gathered to watch the fun.

'You owe me three hundred dollars,' Bat told the spluttering Ritter, 'and, damn it all, if you don't pay up you won't get back in that car alive.'

'This is robbery, you young whelp.' Ritter appealed to the crowd. 'Somebody run and get the marshal. I'm being robbed in broad daylight.'

Bat jammed the gun in Ritter's ribs. 'I'm only collecting what you owe me, and everybody here knows it for a fact. You tried to run out on me and Ed, but you're going to pay off on the barrel-head.'

Ritter shrugged, pulled out a roll of bills tied with a buckskin thong, and peeled off three hundred dollars.

The loafers cheered, the elated Bat jumped off the train, and they all headed for the nearest saloon. The drinks, of course, were on Bat. Anyone big enough to see over the bar was served in those days, especially if he clutched three hundreds dollars in his fist.

This episode marked Bat Masterson's first gunplay. His vigorous method of collecting his debt also earned a certain amount of respect for him when he joined the buffalo hunt of 1872, a stripling among a hard-bitten and ruthless group of men. The great slaughter of buffalo was just then approaching its gory climax, covertly encouraged by the Government, which correctly and coldly foresaw that the day the buffalo herds were killed off would be the day those Indians who were still warlike would be forced to seek food and shelter in the reservations.

Bat managed to buy a Sharps rifle with his hundred-dollars-a-day earnings as a buffalo hunter, but he was not allowed to keep it for long. One day, alone on the prairie, he was approached by five braves of Bear Shield's tribe. They looked peaceable enough, and it had been agreed among the hunters that they should avoid trouble with the Indians, never fire unless fired upon. The braves approached in all amiability, but once they were close the smiles vanished. One of the bucks held Bat at bay with a lance while the others stripped him of rifle and revolver. It was bad enough to be disarmed without putting up a fight, but one of the braves added injury to insult by inflicting a smashing blow on his forehead with the rifle barrel. The braves rode off, leaving Bat with blood dripping in his eyes. He stumbled back to the hunters' camp and proposed that they help him hunt down the Cheyennes.

'The hell with that,' the leader of the outfit said. 'I'm in favour of high-tailing it for Dodge. There might be war parties out all over the plains.'

The hunters and their wagons pulled out that night for Dodge, sixty miles to the north.

Bat, nursing his lacerated scalp and his sorely bruised pride, rode along with them for a few miles and then slipped away on his own. Bear Shield owed him something—like Ritter—and he planned to collect it.

Before dawn he located Bear Shield's pony herd, and an hour later he was headed for Dodge with a fine bunch of stolen horseflesh. The ponies, almost forty of them, brought him twelve hundred dollars in Dodge. Bat felt that was fair recompense for a rifle, a revolver, and a gash on his forehead.

He returned to the buffalo range, joining the hunters on the Salt Fork of the Arkansas, and there he met Wyatt Earp for the first time. Years later all that Earp could remember of that first meeting

92

was that Bat was homesick. Bat, however, would never forget the kindliness with which Earp treated him, nor the impression made on him by the tall, blue-eyed, and steadfast man six years his senior. Bat was particularly impressed by the fact that Earp did not brag and bluster, like the other hunters.

Naturally an exuberant fellow, Bat made a conscious effort to pattern himself after Earp, cultivating a quietly confident manner and learning to hold his tongue. Men like Earp, who were widely respected, he observed, were not given to much pointless conversation.

This admiration of Earp, however, did not extend to being a teetotaller. In that winter encampment Bat learned how to drink in a hardy school indeed.

In the spring of 1874, although barely twenty years old, Bat Masterson was accounted a veteran plainsman and hunter. That spring, in Dodge City, he joined up with an expedition organized by several merchants to strike deep into Indian territory in pursuit of the southward-receding buffalo herds decimated by three years of all-out slaughter above and below the Arkansas.

This further encroachment on the Indians' sacred hunting grounds promised a lot more trouble than any previous forays. According to the Medicine Lodge treaty between the Government and the Indians, the Arkansas was to be the 'deadline', with the buffalo country to the south reserved to the Indians. Now, prodded along by profit-hungry merchants, the hunters planned to plunge far south of that deadline, through the Indian Nations, across the Cimarron, down to the Canadian River, in the Panhandle of Texas.

Bat Masterson, at twenty, was the youngest member of the party. The next youngest and his particular friend was Billy Dixon, who later said he 'never knew anyone that loved practical joking' more than Bat.

Bat looked as harum-scarum as he behaved. He had a mop of black hair with oddly contrasting light-grey eyes that danced with devilry and merriment. He was of medium height, slender but wiry, strong, and resilient. In store clothes and with his hair slicked down, he was described as one of the handsomest young men on the frontier. But it was his slate-grey eyes that attracted attention.

93

Gunfighters came in all shapes, sizes, and temperaments, but almost invariably they had blue eyes. Billy Dixon further noted that for all his fun-loving tendencies Bat was 'a chunk of steel', and anybody who struck him in those days drew fire.

Much of Bat Masterson's life makes him appear like the hero of a picturesque novel. Some of his best friends were murderers and ruffians of the gaudiest hue, and the atmosphere in which he lived for many years was compounded of violence, chicanery, greed, and ruthless devotion to the laws of survival. He never apologized for his friends, and the murky moral climate suited him, but he often seemed to be keeping one foot in heaven.

On the night of June 26, 1874, the buffalo hunters were attacked by Cheyennes and Billy Dixon was killed. It was a terrible battle but Bat escaped without a scratch. In time the battle itself became a rather dim memory to Bat—there was so much other and more personal violence in his life—but he never forgot the dying face of Billy Dixon.

Bat and his companions rode northward through a countryside stiff with terror over the worst Indian outbreak since the Civil War. They reached Dodge without even catching sight of a hostile, but most of the ranchers, hunters, and traders had cleared out for the nearest post of the United States Cavalry. Dodge was in a state of alarm over the border war. The merchants wore long faces and the buffalo-slaughtering trade was at a standstill.

Although several of Bat's fellow adventurers bought tickets on the first train for the East, Bat thought he should stick around for a while. Pride wouldn't let him go home broke, and staring at the rump of a plough horse seemed as unattractive as ever. So he found himself among the unemployed. He had plenty of company that summer, following the depression of 1873. Buffalo-hunting was suspended until the Indians returned to their reservations.

Bat did not fancy a town job such as counter-jumping in one of the stores—too tame for a fellow who had seen the Indians charging out of the dawn, and had been acclaimed as a hero of that battle. But one could not eat congratulations.

The only occupation that offered employment of his unique talents now was scouting for the Army, which was preparing large-scale punitive operations against the tribes. At the invitation of

Colonel Nelson A. Miles, Bat signed on as a civilian scout at Fort Dodge, and was sent to the Texas Panhandle.

After many months of meritorious service as a scout, Bat Masterson limped back to Dodge City in the summer of 1876. In his Texas Panhandle encounters he had acquired some smashed bones in his pelvis that would always give him trouble and cause him to limp slightly, but there was still pride in the way he walked and held himself.

He was a gaudy figure when he stepped along Front Street wearing gold-mounted spurs, a crimson Mexican sash, a red silk neckerchief, a grey sombrero with a rattlesnake band, silver-plated and ivory-handled revolvers, silver-studded belt and holster. Out of earshot the wisecrackers along Front Street said any prospective adversary would be blinded by a mere glimpse of the frontier dandy.

Soon after his arrival he was offered a job as a peace officer. The city marshal was Larry Deger, a political type with little taste for the rigours of keeping order in a wild trail-town, but the operating head of Dodge City's law enforcement was Wyatt Earp, the assistant marshal. Earp, remembering Bat as a cool-headed youngster among the buffalo hunters a few years before, put him on the force as assistant marshal.

From the start, Bat was an easy-going enforcer of law and order, refusing to take a man in unless he was definitely out of hand —invariably from the effects of 'forked lightning' sold as whisky— and a menace to himself and others.

Tact was a mighty useful and inordinately rare quality in Dodge City in the roaring 'seventies. There were more hot tempers, touchy dispositions, and ancient grievances rubbing up against each other in that trail-town, once the Santa Fe Railroad hooked up with the intersection of cattle trails and the Arkansas River near Dodge, than in any other known district. Everybody had a grudge and an acute sense of pride. It was a hardcase town in a hardcase country.

Bat Masterson was one of the few peace officers in Western history who entered a sheriff's election through the jailhouse door.

Early in 1877 he plied his trade as a gambler in Dodge and elsewhere, joining briefly in a stampede towards the scene of South Dakota gold strikes, halting in Cheyenne instead, and enjoying a fine run of luck at the tables. He lingered so long in Cheyenne that he

95

decided the best claims around Deadwood would already be staked. Besides, he had already absorbed a lesson most gold-rushers learned only through brutal experience: the best pickings were to be found not in the ephemeral veins of ore in the earth, but in other men's pockets.

While returning from Cheyenne to Dodge that spring, Bat ran into Wyatt Earp in a Nebraska crossroads settlement. Earp remarked that he had just been offered the marshal's post in Dodge, since Larry Deger had been eased out of office. The saloon-keepers of Dodge wanted a hardboiled marshal to crack down on lawlessness that summer, when two hundred thousand head of cattle would be coming up the trail from Texas, and with them more than two thousand rumbustious cowhands. Earp suggested that Bat run for sheriff of Ford County, of which Dodge City was the county seat, that autumn, but Bat shook his head at the idea. The prospect of taking the Texans over the gaming tables was much more pleasing than protecting the Dodge City saloons and citizens on a sheriff's pay.

But a street brawl, in which Bat intruded himself in a way that clearly showed he held the majesty of the law in no great esteem, was paradoxically the means of changing Bat's mind.

He was strolling along Main Street shortly after his return to Dodge when he noticed a commotion in which Marshal Larry Deger, whom he regarded as an overblown slob, and a little fellow known as Bobby Gill were the principal figures. Gill, who was slightly wobble-headed, was capering about and jeering at the twenty-two-stone marshal. Deger announced he was taking Gill in on a charge of disturbing the peace. Gill declared this a violation of the right of free speech. The marshal began kicking Gill in the direction of the lock-up.

Bat, quite forgetting his background and training as a lawman, rushed to the prisoner's aid. He clamped an armlock on Deger, who outweighed him by more than ten stone, and allowed Gill to scamper away to temporary freedom. Deger then began grappling with his ex-deputy. The marshal, unable to cope with the wiry and infuriated—and possibly half-intoxicated—Bat Masterson, yelled for help. Deputy Marshal Joe Mason snatched Bat's revolver out of its holster. Seeing Bat without his gun gave half a dozen bystanders

96

courage to help subdue him. They held Bat while Deger pistol-whipped him until blood spurted. Even so, it took Deger, Mason, and all their helpers to drag Bat to the jail. Next day he was hauled into court before his old friend Judge Frost and fined twenty-five dollars for fracturing the 'peace' of Dodge City's uproarious saloon and red-light district. Bobby Gill was arrested during the night, and made a remorseful plea before the judge: 'Jesus Christ died for sinners just as me!' Judge Frost was so touched he let Gill off with a five-dollar fine.

A few days later the Dodge City Council showed its sympathy for Bat Masterson by ordering that the fine be remitted.

Somehow this incident convinced the Republicans of Ford County that Bat was the man for the sheriff's office, particularly since Larry Deger, being detached from his marshal's star, was running for sheriff as the nominee of the Democrats.

There were two schools of thought in Dodge regarding how severely the laws should be enforced. The saloon-keepers and smaller merchants wanted property and the wilder visitors segregated south of the Santa Fe. They naturally favoured stern treatment of Texans who felt the urge to hurrah the town. On the other hand, the big store-owners, who handled the large transactions with cattle barons and trail bosses and had become their personal friends, felt the men who brought prosperity to Dodge should be treated more hospitably.

Enough of both factions believed Bat was the man to wear the sheriff's badge. They knew he could be tough, but preferred not to be. Bat agreed to run for sheriff, if for no other reason than to beat Deger out of the job. At the same time he bought a piece of the Lone Star Dance Hall with his winnings at Cheyenne, so he would not suffer financially from assuming public office.

It was a close election. The town was pretty well divided on the subject of Masterson *versus* Deger. Deger had more political influence, Masterson more general popularity. Bat was elected by a margin of three votes in November 1877 for a two-year term.

Bat would have been entirely happy that autumn of 1877 but for the presence of his brother Ed, who had returned to Dodge during the summer and signed on as a deputy marshal. Bat liked having Ed around—he probably loved his brother more than anyone else in the world—but not as a peace officer. Ed just wasn't cut out for it. He was gentle, easy-going, liked everyone, and was liked by everyone who knew him longer than a minute.

Despite Bat's warnings to him that he was no gunfighter, Ed had a run-in with a gunslinger on the night of April 9, 1878, and was fatally wounded. He died in Bat's arms as the latter wept like a child.

Life never looked quite so good to Bat Masterson after that April night his brother was killed. Nothing ever hit him so hard as his brother's death, and nothing ever would.

Bat never did have any time for politics, and he couldn't keep it out of the sheriff's office, hard as he tried. Near the end of his term he came to the conclusion that it was time to move on, especially as his fellow citizens in Dodge City had shown a disappointing preference for beer and bartenders over all-out law enforcement. Bat took his leave of Dodge City with a certain amount of regret—it was the place where he achieved youthful fame—but he would be back soon enough and his guns would be speaking for him in another defence of the family honour.

Tombstone seemed the place to go. That little hellhole in Arizona was reported to be bursting with easy money, violence, and opportunity for the quick-witted.

Tombstone was in its uproarious heyday when Bat appeared there in 1881. Wyatt Earp, his brothers Virgil and Morgan, and Doc Holliday were already established there.

Tombstone attracted the high-rollers, not only because of the proximity of fabulous silver mines in the vicinity, but because it had natural advantages for men who lived outside the law.

Bat's stay in Tombstone was comparatively short—he decided that Trinidad, Colorado, offered greater opportunities to a man of his talents. The day after his arrival there he pinned on the badge of a deputy sheriff of Las Animas County, and later served as city marshal of Trinidad.

Not nearly so lively as Dodge City, Trinidad was determined to keep the lawless element under control, which probably explains the thousand-dollars-per-month salary paid to Bat Masterson as the chief law enforcement officer.

When Bat left Trinidad in the mid-eighties for livelier scenes and more lucrative opportunities he made his home base in Denver, but wandered through the Western Border towns and mining camps for several years as a free-lance gambler. Occasionally he would take on an assignment to restore or preserve the peace. In the meantime, of course, he was always ready to rescue a friend or take a hand in straightening out the civic affairs of Dodge City. In appreciation, the citizens of Dodge during the Fourth of July celebration in 1885, voted Bat 'the most popular man in Dodge City', and awarded him a gold-headed cane, which he carried for many years. Many duplicates of this cane were made, which Bat presented to friends, even to an Indian chief with whom he palavered, and to Governors and United States Senators—unto this day it is his symbol, his trademark. He became an adept in using the cane as a secondary weapon—it bruised, but it did not kill.

For several years Bat continued his stern supervision over Dodge City, and was practically a commuter between there and Colorado. In 1884 he decided to start his own newspaper in Dodge, which he called *Vox Populi*. It did not survive its first edition, but Bat did, which was more than some people expected, considering the things he printed about some of the citizens.

Then the temperance movement hit Dodge, and Bat Masterson jumped into the controversy with both feet and became involved on both sides before it was over. The following spring Bat did a complete and unexplained flipflop. He became a convert to the prohibition cause, and fought just as hard to close Dodge's saloons as he had campaigned less than a year earlier to keep them open. Perhaps he had gone on the wagon himself—he occasionally forswore hard liquor and apparently became as insufferable as most drinkers while on the sarsaparilla—and like all converts wanted to carry others with him.

A legendary figure like Bat Masterson gathers an amazing assortment of untruth by would-be historians and mouth-to-mouth gossips. Bat did not escape this hero-worshipping process of distortion. He was widely credited with killing between twenty and thirty men in gunfights. The actual number, to his eternal credit, was only three. Unable to dissuade the legend-makers, he actually handed out guns with twenty-odd notches to souvenir-hunters who wanted to buy 'the gun you killed all those men with', and took his friends out to buy a drink with the proceeds.

Bat Masterson was no superman who believed that his six-shooter placed him above natural and human law. It can be said that he never killed anyone except in defence of himself or a friend.

Since he and his associates lived by the gun, it might be well to examine the qualities which made Bat shoot better than the next man when it came to a showdown with a Colt .45. To the young and inexperienced gunfighters, he had a masterly standard little discourse on the subject:

The main thing is to shoot first and never miss.

Never try to run a bluff with a six-gun. Many a man has been buried with his boots on because he foolishly tried to scare someone by reaching for his hardware. Always remember that a six-shooter is made to kill the other fellow with, and for no other reason on earth. So always have your gun loaded and ready, and never reach for it unless you are in dead earnest and intend to kill the other fellow.

A lot of inexperienced fellows try to aim a six-shooter by sighting along the barrel, and they try to shoot the other man in the head. Never do that. If you have to stop a man with a gun, grab the stock of your six-shooter with a death-grip that won't let it wobble, and try to hit him just where the belt buckle would be. That's the broadest target from head to foot.

If you point at something, you don't raise your finger to level of the eye and sight along it; you simply point, by instinct, and your finger will always point straight. So you must learn to point the barrel of your six-shooter by instinct. If you haven't that direction instinct born in you, you will never become an expert with the six-gun.

The qualities a man needed to qualify as a man-killing expert with the revolver, Bat Masterson believed, were courage, skill at handling his weapon, and, not the least, steadiness, the ability and coolness to make the first shot.

Like most professionals, Bat had little respect for trick shooting when it came to a showdown. It was all right for exhibitions and friendly contests, but not when facing an opponent.

In 1890 Bat became associated with Ed Chase's elaborate Palace gambling hall on Blake Street, in Denver. He managed the burlesque troupe housed in the Palace Theatre, a sort of dream job, considering the fact that some of the most beautiful women west of Chicago were cavorting there.

Bat Masterson selected his own wife from among the ladies of the Palace ensemble. She was a blonde song-and-dance girl named Emma Walters, a native of Philadelphia, and a comparative veteran of show business. Bat was thirty-seven and his bride thirty-four when they were married on November 21, 1891. Emma realized she was marrying a sporting man, who slept days and was out on the town from sunset to dawn. She was content to stay in the background while Bat lived in the limelight. Since the marriage lasted until the day he died, two months short of their thirtieth wedding anniversary, it may be presumed that she was able to adjust herself to Bat's night-roaming proclivities. The marriage was childless.

A few months after they were married Bat gave up the job of managing the Palace burlesque troupe. He went to Creede as manager of a gambling house and saloon. Emma had given up her career and was pleased with the change. Bat was riding the water wagon with a bridegroom's good intentions, and devoted most of his time to business.

During a period of discontent Bat decided to enter boxing promotion. Prizefighting had been his favourite sport for a long time. Perhaps it came closest to the hand-to-hand combats of his youth. All other sports seemed effete by comparison.

Never having been a boxer, and having preferred to use his cane instead of his fists when dealing with unruly drunks as a peace officer, Bat acquired a considerable knowledge of boxing as a second and a referee. He was in Jake Kilrain's corner when Kilrain lost the heavyweight championship to John L. Sullivan in New Orleans. But he was far from infallible in picking winners. He dropped a large bet on Kilrain against John L. He went broke backing Charlie Mitchell in the latter's fight against James J. Corbett. And he was anything but prophetic in predicting the outcome of the fighter in Carson City, Nevada, between the graceful and spectacular Gentleman Jim Corbett and the small, angular Bob Fitzsimmons.

Bat was discomfited in pride and pocketbook by the spectacle of Corbett, the old dancing master, going down under the sharp-shooting fists of the bald Australian.

What may have impelled Bat to enter fight promotion was the threat that Soapy Smith, one of the old West's most notorious crooks, would take over and make a travesty of a sport that Bat regarded with a certain primitive reverence. Soapy, in fact, did take a fling at matchmaking, and the result was almost disastrous enough to ruin the fight game for ever in Denver.

As an aftermath, the Colorado Athletic Association was organized on April 9, 1899. Less than a month later Otto Floto, the sports editor of the *Denver Post*, used the influence he had acquired in that position, and his closeness to the two powerful political men who published the *Post*, to freeze out competition to himself as promoter.

Bat found that being a fight promoter was a great deal more complicated than merely signing up pugs and counting the box-office receipts. In the first place, prizefighting was illegal in Colorado, and the promoter had to go through the motions of obtaining an injunction to prevent the Denver Fire and Police Commission from interfering with the fight. The commissioners, mostly staunch sporting men themselves, never opposed the injunction.

Floto, by making every use of the powerful influence of his employers, F. G. Bonfils and Harry Tammen, took every unfair advantage of Bat he could in his effort to control the business. The feud produced legislation which resulted in breaking both Floto and Masterson.

At the turn of the century Bat was forty-six years old, broke, ill-fitted for the pursuit of any career outside gambling and the sporting life.

Theodore Roosevelt, then President of the United States, had met Bat on one of his Western tours. Hearing through mutual friends that Bat needed a job, he offered him the post of United States Marshal for the State of Oklahoma. Bat's refusal was one of the sadder verbal mementoes of the old West:

I am not the man for the job. Oklahoma is still woolly, and if I were marshal some youngster would want to try to put me out because of my reputation. I would be a bait for grown-up kids who had fed on dime novels. I would have to kill or be killed. No sense to that. I have taken my guns off, and I don't ever want to put them on again.

Bat brooded over the way Otto Floto had taken advantage of him. One evening in July he trailed the oversized Floto to a café at Sixteenth and Champa streets, near the *Denver Post* building. When Floto emerged there was a tangle, Bat using the gold-headed cane he carried to good advantage. Floto thought it best to run, and, big as he was, outdistanced Bat. However, Bat had managed to give him a good beating with his cane.

As a result of this escapade Bat was forced to leave Denver, due to the pressure exerted by Bonfils and Tammen. He went home to pack, and told his wife he was going East and would send for her. Nobody went to the depot with him except two detectives who had been detailed to see that he got on the first train out of town.

Bat Masterson arrived in New York City early in June 1902, disillusioned with the West and eager to test the truth of the claim that no metropolis in the world knows better how to treat a celebrity, no matter what his leasehold to fame. He liked the looks of the big town.

Three days after his arrival he stood on the corner of West 69th Street and Columbus Avenue talking to two card-sharks he had known in Dodge City, and whom he had met again by chance. The long arm of the law reached and grabbed the three of them. They were charged with fleecing an elder of the Mormon Church on a train which had arrived in New York that day. It was a bum rap for Bat, as he hadn't even been on the train, and had just run into the two crooks.

He was quickly released when his New York friends heard of his arrest. But the New York Police were not quite through with him. They had little affection for Westerners who felt naked without their personal armament. On June 15 Bat was picked up again, and charged with carrying a concealed weapon. This time he complained to a reporter of the *New York World*.

'Why, there's thousands of jokers running wild in New York carrying guns bigger than mine, and not a word said about it. Why did I carry it? Well, I'm accustomed to carrying bunches of money in the night, when good people are asleep.'

The reporter made a good story out of it, and again Bat was turned loose. This time he decided to hang up his gun belt for good.

President Theodore Roosevelt, in Washington, read the story in the papers and decided Bat needed a job to keep him out of mischief.

The President telegraphed Bat, offering him the post of United States Marshal for the southern district of New York. This time Bat accepted. It was a political sinecure, a desk job, and there was no chance of running into trigger-happy youngsters such as abounded in the West. The marshal's job made Emma Masterson happy too, for it had the solid virtues of a Government salary and daytime hours. Bat lost no time in bringing her to New York and finding a suitable apartment.

In exchange for providing him with a place on the Federal payroll, President Roosevelt insisted on Bat coming down to Washington occasionally and talking with him on two of his favourite subjects—the old West and prizefighting.

The visits continued even after Bat resigned as Federal Marshal to enter journalism.

Bat had known the Lewis brothers when they ventured to Dodge City to write Western stories. In New York he renewed the acquaintance. W. E. Lewis provided Bat with a job as sports editor on the *Morning Telegraph*, and the other Lewis brother, Alfred Henry, became Bat's constant companion, chief admirer, and propagandist.

Bat made the transition from Federal Marshal to sports editor of the *Morning Telegraph* with more grace and ease than might be expected. He had long been inclined in that direction, and the job combined his love of sport, particularly boxing, with his flair for expressing himself with the vividness demanded of a sports-writer. It is not easy to take up a new profession when a man is past fifty, but Bat had just written a series on gunfighters for *Human Life* magazine, which was well received and gave him a certain amount of confidence.

As the years went by Bat was more than satisfied with his life in New York. He no longer felt any overwhelming nostalgia for the West. He had gained a wide reputation for his fearless writing. Four-square to all the winds that blew, he despised hypocrisy and dishonesty, and he had a forceful way of expressing his feelings.

By the time the 1920's rolled around, Bat and the men of his generation were trying to adjust themselves to a strange new world. Prohibition had come, and Bat could not give his approval to the speakeasy, the blind tiger, and the beer flat which had succeeded the saloons. The tommy-gun had taken the place of the six-shooter. Well-organized gangsters had supplanted the badmen, the horse thieves, the cattle rustlers, and stage robbers of the old days. It was a different world to Bat Masterson.

In 1921 Bat was sixty-seven years old, a gentle old fellow, mellow and good-natured, except when he wrote of the frauds and pretenders of the prize ring.

On October 25, 1921, shortly before noon, Bat strolled up Eighth Avenue from his apartment to the *Morning Telegraph* office and wrote his column for the next day. Fifteen minutes after he finished it he died alone in his office, slumped over his rolltop desk. A more prosaic death scene for a less prosaic man could hardly be imagined. When found, his last column was clutched in his hand.

Bat's death was reported on the front pages of the afternoon editions of the New York papers, one of which said: 'He died at his desk gripping his pen with the tenacity with which he formerly clung to his six-shooter.'

Emma Masterson lived another eleven years, faithful unto eternity. The *New York Herald-Tribune* obituary said of her: 'She remained an obscure figure behind the bright flare of her husband's fame.'

Colt's Army .45-calibre (New Service model of 1909)

5 Henry Starr

Henry Starr has been called by those who should know the most spectacular outlaw who ever operated in the South-west, with the possible exception of Jesse James. Not that Jesse's exploits were more spectacular than Starr's, but he was able to remain out of prison all the years of his bandit career, whereas Henry Starr spent three-fourths of his time behind prison walls.

An uncanny marksman and a man with a strange sense of honour, Henry was known as 'The Bearcat' because of his cunning and his forthright courage. Yet a large share of the notoriety which surrounded this gunman was probably due to the fact that he bore the same name as Bella Starr. Indeed, there were stories that he was her son and some said he was her brother-in-law. Actually Henry was no blood relation to Bella Starr at all. He was Sam Starr's cousin, and as such a cousin-in-law to the infamous Bella.

Henry's career as probably America's most spectacular bank robber didn't actually begin until four years after Bella was shot in the back in 1889. He was the only man who ever successfully carried off two robberies in the same town on the same day. That feat had been tried unsuccessfully, and with dire results, by the Daltons at Coffeyville, Kansas, years before Starr did it in 1915. And if ever a man died with his boots on, in the popular phrase, Starr did. He was mortally wounded trying to carry out a bank robbery in the grand tradition of the Western frontier as late as 1921, three years after the end of World War I. It was the last of the outlaw-breed bank robberies, and Starr was probably the last of the breed.

Henry was a man of vast personal incongruities. Although he made no excuse for his devastating career as an outlaw, other than blaming a mistake by the law when he was a youth, in his personal habits Starr was a man of strong moral convictions. He was not addicted to liquor, tobacco, coffee, or tea, and was the son of well-to-do parents. Although he stole thousands of dollars during his long career, he died a pauper. His only assets were his burial expenses, paid years before to a Tulsa, Oklahoma, undertaker. At the time he said that he was certain he would die while performing some robbery, and he did not wish to bring unnecessary hardship to those he left behind.

Henry Starr first saw the light of day on December 2, 1873, at Fort Gibson, Indian Territory. He was the son of George (Hop) Starr, a half-breed Cherokee, and Mary Scott, a quarter-blood. He attended the Cherokee Indian Mission until his eleventh birthday, when he left school following the death of his father. At first Henry attempted to shoulder the responsibility of taking care of his mother and two brothers. Two years later his mother remarried, and Henry, after trying in vain to get along with his stepfather, finally left home and became a cowboy on one of the large cattle ranches then scattered over the Cherokee Nation.

Although it is known that Henry Starr and Bella Starr had a brief alliance in the late 'eighties, Henry never ran foul of the law until 1892, when he was arrested on a charge of horse-stealing. According to Starr's own story the arrest was an unfair one and embittered him to the point where he turned completely to a life of crime. Starr claimed that the horse in question was a stray and wandered into the pasture of the ranch, where the youngster was working. He watched it for several days and when nobody claimed the animal he mounted it and rode into Nowata. The owner of the animal saw him, recognized the horse, and had Henry arrested as a thief. Starr spent several months in jail before the trial, at which he was acquitted.

'When they let me out I was bitter against the world,' Starr said. 'I decided that if they sent people to jail when they had violated no law they couldn't do more to a real criminal. Having been branded a criminal, I thought I might as well be one in fact.

'I was only a kid, and father and mother had brought me up to think it was an awful disgrace to be in jail. They chained me to a bed that time. That was a bad thing to do to a kid. I was innocent. When I was released I felt that I might as well be dead as disgraced. I came out of that jail with blood in my eye.'

Henry Starr was nineteen at the time, and from that day on he was an outlaw. An incurable gambler, Starr had disastrous luck at cards. He regularly turned over every penny he made or stole to those with whom he gambled, and yet he never held up a gambling table—another example of his strange sense of honour. Henry robbed his first bank at Caney, Kansas, in 1893, and after that kept his purse full from the proceeds of attacks on small country banks.

'Guess Henry just figured that the banks owed him what he could take from them, is the way I look at it,' remarked an old-time friend of the outlaw. 'I don't believe he thought it was wrong. I know he thoroughly enjoyed raiding. He's told me of how he laughed inwardly until he could hardly control himself at the enormous fright some victim banker would show when Starr and his men would step in and take charge of all the loose currency with the "Hands up and hands steady" that Starr always sung out.'

That was Henry, a recklessly bold, practical joker at heart; but a gunman at hand. His complete underestimation of the dangers involved in his illegal occupation accounted for Henry's somewhat surprising record as a highwayman. He was wounded on several occasions and was captured several times. These misfortunes didn't seem to provide any serious deterrent to his choice of career. He kept right on holding up banks—even after he was paroled from prison sentences on two occasions, once when Teddy Roosevelt was President of the United States.

During the early part of his career Henry was implicated in cattle and horse thefts, the robbery of the Carter store in Nowata, the Schufeldt store in Lenapah, the stick-up of the depot at Nowata and of the M.K.T. train at Adair. In 1892 the express office at Nowata was robbed by masked men who made their getaway on horseback. One of the robbers' mounts bolted into a wire fence and its rider was thrown. The horse ran away and was found later wearing a saddle Henry Starr had borrowed from a friend.

A few days later Henry rode into Lenapah, in Nowata County, and was recognized by Floyd Wilson, a deputy marshal and special officer for the Iron Mountain Railroad. The men rode up to each other on horseback, Wilson pulling his Winchester in a gesture for Henry to surrender. The rifle jammed and Henry pulled out his six-gun, calling to the officer to give up, that he didn't want to shoot him. Wilson was game, and believed he could get his man. He pulled his revolver. Starr's strange sense of fair play prevailed. Even though his pistol was already drawn Henry allowed Wilson to get in the first shot. The bullet whizzed past him and Starr answered with a bullet through Wilson's heart.

It was two years before the law caught up with Henry, and during that time he fashioned a career which was fairly remarkable for the times. In January 1893 he and several others shot up the town of Choteau, Indian Territory, robbed two general stores and the depot. A few days later they robbed the general store and depot at Inola, Indian Territory. On March 25 Henry tried his first bank robbery. With a friend, Frank Chaney, he stuck-up the Caney Valley National Bank and got away with 4,900 dollars. His notoriety spread, and by April dozens of lesser-known bandits were offering him their services.

On May 5 the gang held up the Katy passenger train at Pryor Creek, getting 6,000 dollars and a consignment of diamonds. It was during this robbery that Starr's courtship with Mary Morrison, a young lady travelling from Nowata to Joplin, began in a singularly spectacular and romantic fashion. Starr was standing on the platform of the first coach in order to direct the operations of his men. A young woman, wild with terror, rushed past him and leaped into the darkness. The work of robbing the train took about half an hour, after which Starr and his men rode off through the woods. Half a mile from the scene the desperadoes came on the girl, and the poor thing was half crazy with fright. Starr carried the near-petrified young woman to the outlaw camp, and the following day he sent her with one of his men as an escort to catch the train for Joplin, Missouri. Before she left the camp Starr told her he would come to visit her. A few weeks later, under the name of Frank Jackson,

Henry came to Joplin. A brief courtship followed, and in several weeks the two were engaged, but they did not marry until after Henry's release from the Columbus, Ohio, Penitentiary some years later.

On June 6 the Starr gang pulled a daring hold-up, riding into Arkansas to rob the bank at Bentonville of 11,500 dollars. After that the band broke up, and Starr, with the law in close pursuit, met his sweetheart in the Osage Hills, and they started for Emporia, Kansas, where they expected to take a train for California and the start of a new life. With them was 'Kid' Wilson, another desperado whom Henry had come to know since the start of his wild and lawless escapades.

At Fort Smith, Arkansas, the alert deputies of 'Hanging Judge' Parker spotted the two outlaws and they were captured. There was more than forty thousand dollars in the wagon. Starr was tried for the murder of Wilson, convicted, and sentenced to be hanged. Prominent members of the Cherokee Nation, working with Starr's wife and mother, managed to put off the execution for a period of two years, and succeeded in getting Henry a new trial. He was sentenced to thirteen years in the Federal Penitentiary at Columbus, Ohio. While waiting to be taken to Columbus a strange incident took place in the Fort Smith jail, one which indicates yet again that Henry Starr had an uncanny sense of justice.

Occupying a nearby cell in the jail was Crawford Goldsby, better known as 'Cherokee Bill', one of America's most vicious murderers. Cherokee Bill was born at Fort Concho, Texas, February 8, 1876, of mixed Negro, Indian, and white blood. His father was a member of the famous Tenth Cavalry, coloured, of the United States Army, and was of Mexican extraction with white and Indian blood mixed in. His mother, Ellen Beck, was half Negro, a fourth Cherokee, and a fourth white. Cherokee Bill was educated at Cherokee, Kansas, and at the Catholic Indian School at Carlisle, Pennsylvania, until he was twelve. His parents separated soon after his birth. By the time he was eighteen Goldsby was a burly, mean, undisciplined trouble-maker.

After shooting a Negro named Jack Lewis, Goldsby, and two other tough customers, Jim and Bill Cook, escaped into Indian Territory and in the spring of 1894 got a woman named Crittenden to draw their share of money being paid by the Federal Government to the Indians of the Cherokee Strip. Soon after receiving the money they went on a monumental bender. Two nights later a sheriff's posse finally trapped them in a house, and in the ensuing fracas Sequoyah Houston, who had a Cherokee warrant to arrest Cook on a larceny charge, was killed. Following the battle, in which Goldsby escaped, one of the members of his makeshift gang referred to him as 'Cherokee Bill' and the name stuck.

Soon afterwards the famous Cook Gang was organized. Its members were Bill Cook, Henry Munson, Curtis 'Chicken' Gordon, Sam Williams, known as the 'Verdigras Kid', and Cherokee Bill Goldsby. In 1894 the gang robbed the Schufeldt store in Lenapah, and Bill shot an onlooker at a window across the street from the scene because the man 'was annoying him'.

Goldsby was finally captured by two deputies, Isaac Rogers and Clint Scales, after they first attempted to drug him with morphine-loaded whisky, and then knocked him cold with their pistols. A huge crowd attended the trial, which opened in February 1895 before Hanging Judge Parker. Goldsby was accused of killing thirteen men.

Cherokee Bill was awaiting his trip to the gallows when Henry Starr was confined in a nearby cell. On July 26, 1895, a gun was smuggled into the jail. The weapon was tied at the end of a long pole and thrust through the window of Bill's cell during the night. Bill later said the gun was supplied by Ben Howell, believed to have been a confederate of the Doolin and Dalton gangs.

On the afternoon of July 26 a guard named Lawrence Keating came in to lock the cells following a free period in the jail and found Cherokee Bill's foot blocking his cell door. As he leaned to move the badman out of the way Bill shot him dead. Then the lobo Indian went on a rampage, exchanging shots with the guards and gobbling like a turkey every time he fired. He finally backed into his own cell, from where he could fire without exposing himself. The guards retired to discuss the situation. That was when Henry Starr volunteered to disarm the wild man. Without a word he walked down the runway, swung open the door to Cherokee Bill's cage, and entered. The officers, safe around the corner, heard only a faint whispering. A few minutes later Starr stepped out, locked the cell, and delivered the badman's gun to the astonished officers. Henry never explained how he had unarmed the vicious Cherokee Bill.

After another trial for the killing of Keating, followed by numerous appeals, Cherokee Bill was finally hanged on March 17, 1896. When he stepped on to the gallows and was asked if he had any last comment to make, Bill's reply was the classic: 'I came here to die, not to make a speech.'

Superstitious persons might be interested in one facet of Cherokee Bill's life. The number 13 appeared with almost supernatural regularity throughout his days. It took Judge Parker 13 minutes to instruct the jury. There were 13 witnesses against Bill, the jury and bailiff numbered 13, and the trial lasted 13 hours. Bill was first sentenced to die on April 13, and the guard was killed on March 26—twice 13. Bill is said to have fired 13 shots during his escape attempt, and there were 13 steps up the gallows the day he was hanged. There were 13 knots in the hangman's noose and the trap was sprung at exactly 2.13 p.m. Also Bill is said to have murdered 13 men.

Starr's heroic act in disarming Cherokee Bill eventually led to his pardon, but he served eight of his thirteen years before that act was brought to the attention of Teddy Roosevelt. During those eight years Henry devoted himself to reading, particularly law books. Upon leaving prison he announced his intention of settling down on his farm near Tulsa and trying to obtain a law degree. During his prison stay Henry had made the acquaintance of Al Jennings, an Oklahoma outlaw, who was also intending to go straight when he was released. Later Starr said his intentions were honest.

'I meant it. That's why I named my son after Roosevelt— Roosevelt Starr.'

In 1907, after he and his wife had lived in Tulsa for a while and successfully operated a real-estate business, the monotony of his everyday existence began to pall on Henry Starr. He moved to Skiatook. Meanwhile Oklahoma became a state, and the Starrs were among the notables at the inauguration of Charles N. Haskell, its first Governor. But Arkansas had not forgotten the Bentonville bank hold-up. When Oklahoma became a state, Arkansas authorities asked that Starr be returned on an indictment. Starr was uneasy while awaiting Haskell's decision. Finally he had a friend call the

Governor's office to find out what that decision was. The friend misunderstood the answer. He thought the secretary had said 'He's granted it' instead of 'He hasn't granted it.'

Starr fled west and joined his old pal Kid Wilson, who also had been released from prison. On Friday, March 13, 1908, the two men robbed the bank in Tyro, Kansas, and escaped. Starr had carried out his operations in his usual daring manner. The bandits fled into the Osage Indian country with a posse in hot pursuit. Women even took part in the chase, telephoning the whereabouts of the outlaws, who had made off with 2,500 dollars. Throughout the day messages poured into the sheriffs' offices.

'The outlaws have just stopped on a hill above our house.'

'The bank robbers just stopped here and asked for a drink of water.'

One posse blundered by accident into the outlaws when they stopped at an oil camp and ordered the cook to prepare dinner. The posse had taken a pack of trail hounds with them, and a hunting horn was dangling from the saddlehorn of one posseman.

'What the hell you fellows want?' Starr asked.

'Why, we're wolf-hunting and we're looking for a bob-tailed hound of mine. Have you seen him?' came the reply.

'Damn you and your bob-tailed hound,' Starr snapped. 'You're after me and you know it. Get their guns, boys.'

Starr's usual good humour and sense of sportsmanship prevailed. After emptying the posse's guns and restoring them to the owners, he recognized one man in the group, A. P. Tullock. This man had been a member of a posse which had captured Starr on a previous occasion. He had sworn to kill Tullock at the time.

'I have a notion to kill you,' Starr said to Tullock as he walked over to him.

'Don't do that without giving him a chance, Henry,' said one of the outlaws who had assisted in the Tyro robbery.

'I guess you're right. Give him a gun and I'll fight it out with him.'

Tullock knew Starr's reputation as a gunman, and begged not to be killed. The genial outlaw finally conceded. In the distance he saw two other riders galloping as though a prairie fire was chasing them.

'Who are those fellows, and what's their hurry?' Starr asked one of the lawmen.

'I don't know anything about them.'

'Better tell me the truth or I'll kill you,' Starr snapped.

The posseman told him one of the riders was a man named Cunningham, and the pair were probably racing to warn the other lawmen scouring the countryside.

Almost smiling, Starr remarked: 'I'm gonna have to kill that Cunningham one of these fine days.'

Before Starr and his men made their getaway the entire area was in an uproar. Posses shot at each other; one account put it this way:

It was reported that natives all along the road were out with corn knives and shotguns and it would be dangerous for a stranger to pass along the highway after the sun had set. Behind every fence post and in every clump of weeds lingered one man or a dozen, ready to shoot down a bank robber or a peaceable citizen without the least provocation.

Henry Starr, however, made a clean getaway. It was remarkable that nobody was killed. But Starr had that reputation. He once claimed he never had killed a man with the exception of Deputy Marshal Wilson, and that is generally conceded to be the truth, with the possible exception of Kid Wilson.

An acquaintance once described Henry's ability with a gun as almost unbelievable. This man was taken to meet Starr in a thicket hideout where Starr was relaxing following a stick-up. They were taking in the sunshine on the bank of a stream, and the heads of turtles bobbed up through the shining surface of the water. The man remarked that he had heard of Starr's ability with a pistol. Without further word Henry stood up, and pulling both guns fired twelve shots, hitting a turtle with every one.

He never seemed to lose his sense of humour either. Once, after robbing a bank and making off with a great deal of paper material by mistake, he commented to a friend: 'These things are of no value to us, but I'd hate to see the farmers have to pay.'

The papers were all mortgages and loan records. Starr went through all the papers and delivered each one personally to the names therein. Tears of gratitude and words of thanks flowed in the wake of Henry's many visits, and as he left each place he remarked: 'Be sure to burn those papers, and if those loan sharks try to get you to sign another, tell them to go to hell.'

On one occasion after robbing a bank in Caney, Kansas, Starr and his band shot craps in a barn all night; then when the sheriff rode into the yard Starr called a temporary truce and walked out, shaking hands warmly, as though they were old pals.

'I'm going to leave here at three o'clock. There are three of us. If you don't want your men hurt you better get them out of the way. When we start we're going through the lines. You tell your men that for me.'

The sheriff told his men, and within five minutes there wasn't a man within rifle range of Henry. At three o'clock he and his men rode away unmolested. On another occasion, when a sheriff's posse was on his trail, friends went to warn him. They found Henry calmly trailing the sheriff.

'If I keep him in front of me all the time I'll know exactly where he is,' Henry commented at their surprise.

In the summer of 1908 Wilson and Starr robbed the Amity, Colorado, bank and escaped. Starr remained within ten miles of the town while the Colorado authorities were scouring the countryside for him. A few months later Starr and Kid Wilson parted company— Starr later telling friends he was afraid Wilson was going beserk and would kill him. Wilson was never seen or heard of again, but in later years Starr is reported as having told a friend: 'Wilson won't bother anyone else.' Wilson's fate is still a matter of conjecture.

After splitting with Wilson, Starr went to Arizona, where he felt he would be safe from the Colorado authorities. Needing money, he wrote to a man he believed was a friend and asked him to dispose of an Indian allotment he had in Tulsa and to send him the money. The trust was misplaced. The real-estate dealer promptly gave the Colorado police Starr's address and Arizona officers arrested Henry. The daring outlaw was captured and returned to Colorado, where in 1909 he was tried and sentenced to twenty-five years in the State Penitentiary.

Henry Starr conducted himself as a model inmate of the prison, finally convincing the warden and others that he was going to give up his outlaw career and live a respectable life. He was a smooth talker, and soon had most of the prison personnel on his side. Henry served only four years, and was pardoned by the Governor in 1913 on the agreement that he would never again set foot in Oklahoma. Here once again is shown Starr's utter contempt for the authorities. He remained in Colorado only a few months and then returned to his home state. Taking the alias of 'R. L. Williams', which was the name of a candidate for Governor, Henry settled in a bungalow at 1534 East Second Street. Gas and light meters were registered to Laura Williams, Starr's wife, as was the telephone. Two doors away lived Jim Woolley, the sheriff of Tulsa County. Next door was the city's largest school and every day at recess children played in the backyard of the noted outlaw.

During this period Al Jennings, who had returned to Oklahoma and settled down after his release from prison, was running for the Democratic gubernatorial nomination against Robert L. Williams, J. B. A. Robertson, Charles West, and Robert Dunlop. Probably to muddle the situation as much as possible for Williams, the favourite candidate, Henry Starr had his alias of R. L. Williams placed on the ticket to help his old pal Jennings. But Robert L. Williams won the election anyway. It was a typical stunt for Henry to pull, however, and many folks got a big laugh out of it in later years.

Many of Starr's close friends believed that during this phase of his career he also directed many of the numerous bank robberies in Oklahoma from his quiet little home in Tulsa. On March 27, 1915, Starr led his men in the most daring robbery of his entire career. The dual attack on the city of Stroud, Lincoln County, Oklahoma, was his masterpiece. Starr later said he planned the robbery for his son's sake.

'I wanted to make a stake for him. I wanted to make a big haul, fix the boy out, and go off somewhere and be forgotten.'

The Stroud hold-ups were daringly planned. The robbers rode into town, tethered their horses to the stockyard fence, left one of their number in charge of the mounts, and then held up and robbed the town's two banks of more than five thousand dollars. As the robbers rushed to make good their escape Paul Curry, a fifteen-year-old boy, ran into a butcher's shop, grabbed a sawed-off rifle, and fired at the bandits. The bullet smacked into Starr's leg, shattering it. Louis Estes, another of the robbers, was shot in the neck and captured. As Starr fell the youth cried: 'Throw away your gun or I'll kill you sure!' Starr complied.

'I am a bank robber and have been caught. That's all there is to say,' Starr shrugged.

Convicted at Chandler, Starr was sentenced to twenty-five years. His life was saved before the trial by the veteran peace officer Bill Tilghman, who quickly quelled a threatened lynching. The remainder of the bandits escaped with the loot and were never caught.

In prison Starr's charm, good nature, and amazing knack of convincing penal authorities of his sincerity once again won him a parole. In 1919 Governor Robertson granted him a pardon. This time the parole petition had on it the signatures of the prosecuting attorney, the judge who presided at the trial, and most of the jurors who convicted him. Starr had convinced the whole group that he was going into the motion-picture business.

'After all, there's more money in the motion-picture business than there is in bank-robbing,' pointed out the Lincoln County prosecutor.

He was right. Starr went into the motion-picture business with great vigour. A company was quickly formed and the first film was a re-enactment of the infamous Stroud robbery complete to the last detail, with Starr playing himself. The picture even included the youth who had shot him. Starr made considerable money out of the picture and was the leading character in several others that followed. George Davis, a motion-picture official in Tulsa, said that Starr received an offer from Hollywood to assist in staging a bank robbery, after which the possibility of engaging him in other Western films was to be considered.

Starr was mulling over the offer when he went to Harrison, Arkansas, to his death. It would seem strange that on the brink of what promised to be a surprising career as a motion-picture actor, Starr would have suddenly turned back to his old habits. But the urge must have been in his blood, and he could not resist it. Davis said that he believed Starr had been engaged in bank-robbing almost from the time he was paroled. While making pictures, Starr visited Chandler and Davenport, Oklahoma. On both occasions the banks there were robbed, although Starr was never even suspected.

On February 18, 1921, Starr entered the People's National Bank in Harrison and ordered the clerk and other people in the building to put up their hands. With him were three confederates. The men were using a car for their getaway. Here Henry Starr was tripped up by a man with masterful coolness, courage, and foresight—enough to match even that of Henry himself. W. J. Meyers, president of the bank, had put a back door in the vault years before on the chance that bank robbers might some day lock employees in the safe. He had also placed a shotgun inside. As Starr was stuffing bags with money, Meyers fired on him from inside the vault. Mortally wounded, Starr toppled over. The three other men, apparently confused, aimed at the cashier, Cleve Coffman, but Starr yelled to them not to shoot anyone. The men made their escape in the car, leaving the wounded robber leader behind.

True to his nature, Starr held no ill-will towards anyone connected with the shooting. Of Meyers he said: 'I do not blame him at all. I would have done the same thing in his place. He was at one end of the game and I at the other, and he won. He has a cool hand.'

Henry Starr seemed in no way ashamed of his profession, but in a message to his son advised the boy to keep on the straight and narrow path; not to try to imitate his father.

The bandit had been shot in the spine, and was paralysed. He asked to see the cashier, and when the youth came in he said: 'You know I saved your life.' Cleve Coffman nodded. He remained with Starr almost until the very end, and the robber gave the cashier his pistol as a souvenir. According to the man whose life Starr had spared, the outlaw stated that he had never killed a man in the course of his career as a bank robber, and had conducted his notorious affairs in the 'whitest manner possible'.

Four days later, on February 22, the amazing career of Henry Starr came to an end. He was buried on February 25, at Dewey, Oklahoma.

Throughout his entire life Starr seems to have been plagued more with the excitement and adventure involved in the robbery of a bank than in the actual riches gained from it. He was constantly entranced with new ideas and schemes for outwitting the law. He even tried camouflage, once painting his horse black and pasting white spots on it, then washing it clean later. He resorted to fake moustaches, shaggy brows and beards, but rarely wore a mask. His inherent sense of fair play is obvious throughout his career. He once wrote a friend:

A man who commits a crime and then shoots an officer who tried to capture him is a fool. The officers never quit hunting you if you kill a man, but they don't pay too much attention if you just rob a bank or stick up a train. While I'm scouting I am going to take good care not to kill a man.

It is also apparent that he tried time and time again to throw off the cloak of outlaw. While in prison in Colorado he said: 'I know I have been a bad man in my days; but I am innocent of a whole lot of these crimes. I believe I will be pardoned out of here in another ten years. Then I can look the whole world in the face and be a man among men.'

But try as he might, it never quite worked out that way for Henry Starr. In all, he served seventeen years and eight months in prison, and he knew the tragedy of his ways. He gave a newspaper-man just before his death what is perhaps a clue to his insatiable appetite for crime:

Once a fellow falls it is hard to rise again. Never let any vice get a firm hold on you as you will not be able to shake it off. One thing leads to another and before you know it you are in too deep to back out. Gambling was my vice. I could never get enough of it and always had to have money, no matter whose it was, to satisfy that awful craving. All young men should know crime is a losing game, no matter who the players may be. I would not take 17,000,000 dollars to again face the agony I have endured.

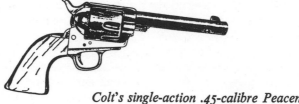

Colt's single-action .45-calibre Peacemaker (1873)

6 Henry Brown

N O ONE knew very much about a young fellow who called himself Henry Brown when he joined the buffalo-hunting party of A. C. Myers in the spring of 1874. Even his birthplace has been a bone of contention these many years. This writer firmly believes that Brown was a native of Rolla, in Phelps County, Missouri, and that he went into Kansas to become a whisky pedlar, then a buffalo hunter.

The Myers wagon train crossed the Arkansas River at Dodge City, Kansas, and made Crooked Creek by sundown, and there went into camp. By the second night they had arrived at the Cimarron River. All the while lithe Henry Brown was doing his chores as one of the members of the band. With him were the noted frontier scout, Billy Dixon, Dutch Henry Born, later to become a notorious rustler, and the youngest of the party was William Barclay (Bat) Masterson.

The scouts reported that a solid mass of shaggy buffalo was on the way north. Myers and some of the men continued until they reached a point about a mile and a half above the ruins of Bent's Fort. They settled down there and began constructing their buildings. Myers chose to build a picket house for his store. A picket house was built by digging a trench and setting upright poles in it. The logs were filled in with adobe mud and grass, as in the log cabins of the pioneers, who chinked the space between the logs with mud.

Henry Brown assisted Jim Hanrahan, a saloon-keeper, to construct his building. They also built another sod house, which became Rath and Wright's store. Soon rumours drifted into camp that the Indians were on the warpath because the hunters had settled at the new Adobe Walls location. Chiefs Quanah Parker, Lone Wolf, White Shield, and Stone Calf called the party invaders of Texas territory and violators of the Medicine Lodge Treaty. Later two hunters named Dudley and Wallace were slain on Chicken Creek. Emanuel Dobbs and his party were attacked near the Salt Ford of the Red Canadian River, south-east of Adobe Walls. Three of them were killed.

On June 27 there were still twenty-eight men and one woman at the Adobe Walls camp. These men had decided to remain and hunt the buffalo. By midnight they had all retired to their bunks, or were sprawled on the ground, for it was a hot sultry night. Suddenly a sharp cracking sound rent the still air. Inside Hanrahan's saloon Henry Brown jumped up.

'It's the ridge pole. Too much earth on the roof. The weight has cracked the ridge pole. Got to prop it up or it will all topple in on us.'

A light was hastily lit and shouts for help soon brought the men to Hanrahan's, and a stout prop was installed in place. Bat Masterson took a careful look at the ridge pole and then looked at Mike Welch, who also was in the saloon when Henry jumped up.

'Henry, you must have been dreaming. That pole is as solid as your own head.'

No sound reason has ever been given regarding this phenomenon, one which saved the lives of all those present. No visible crack was ever found in the ridge pole.

Hanrahan then spoke up.

'Whether the pole was cracked or not, we are all awake, so we might as well get an early start for the hunt.'

Calling Billy Ogg, Hanrahan told him to drive up the horses. Billy Dixon headed for his wagon, which was outside O'Keefe's shop. Henry walked out into the night for a breath of fresh air. He looked to the east, then to the south, where he could see Billy Ogg bringing in the horses. He looked again! Something was moving beyond the horses. Suddenly out of the night came the unmistakable sound of a bugle sounding the charge. This was followed by the shrill war-whoops of Plains Indians, as a war party rushed towards the buildings. Henry Brown, Billy Dixon, and Billy Ogg dashed back into Hanrahan's, shouting a warning as they ran.

Henry Brown hastily tossed up bags of grain to protect the window openings. He then calmly reached for his famous rifle and sent lethal slugs into the Indian ranks. By now all of the hunters present were shooting at the attackers and the first charge of the redskins was blocked, but some of them managed to rush right up to the building and to fire through the windows. Although every pane of glass was broken not one of the hunters was wounded.

At a picket corral to the north two brothers named Shadler were killed and scalped.

Time after time the massed Indians charged, riding up to the buildings, where they hammered furiously against doors and window-frames with their tomahawks. Like bees they swarmed around the thick sod walls, while the steady and devastating fire of the defenders toppled warrior after warrior from his pony. Henry Brown made every shot count, and once an enemy was struck by a heavy Sharps bullet he seldom got up to rejoin the fight.

In the ranks of the Indians was a renegade bugler, who summoned the braves to the attack. Ex-soldiers among the hunters interpreted the calls and warned the inmates, who then met every charge with deadly results.

Henry Brown and Bat Masterson stood shoulder to shoulder at a window, shooting until the space outside their window was so littered with corpses that fresh attackers could not draw near without trampling the bodies.

By noon the Indians had withdrawn and confined their tactics to circling the valley out of rifle range.

Morning of the second day still found the Indians keeping their distance. The hunters spent that day burying the dead Indians as well as the two white men who had been killed.

'Our ammunition is running mighty low,' said Henry Brown. 'If those devils find that out we're goners.'

The third day arrived with the Indians still congregated on the high bluff to the east across the valley, a distance of almost a mile. It seemed to all present that they were well out of range of even the powerful Sharps rifles. Others maintained that the Sharps would send a lethal charge that far. One of the Indians could be seen fairly well, and he was making grotesque signs at the white hunters. Billy Dixon was conceded to be the best shot present, and then Henry Brown. It was finally decided that Dixon should 'waste' a bullet on the taunting redskin.

Taking careful aim, Dixon dropped the hammer. The roar of the big .50-calibre rifle was immediately followed by the Indian diving headlong from his pony's back. Later the distance was measured off and proved to be 1,538 yards. This was indeed a record shot, even among the dead-shot hunters.

This fantastic feat discouraged further attack, and Quanah Parker and his allies withdrew their forces.

Any record of the movements of Henry Brown after the Adobe Walls fight until 1877 has been lost. In that year the young and daring rifleman arrived at old Fort Griffin, located on the Clear Fork of the Brazos River.

It was plain that the days of the buffalo hunter were over. The depleted herds offered little or no recompense for a man's labour. Henry decided to try his fortune in another direction. At Fort Griffin he learned of the trouble brewing in Lincoln County, New Mexico, and soon was to become embroiled in the bloody struggle between the paid gunhands of the McSween-Chisum gang and those of the Murphy-Dolan faction.

Henry listened closely. His wide-spreading ears twitched and his blue eyes sparked as he learned of the high wages being paid gunmen in Lincoln County. He quickly bid his friends adieu and hit the trail for New Mexico.

Lincoln, New Mexico, was an armed camp when he arrived. Riff-raff and gunslingers from all over the South-west had migrated into Lincoln County, seeking both excitement and the high wages being offered by both feuding sides.

John Simpson Chisum, Alexander McSween, his attorney, and an Englishman named Tunstall were at dagger's point with the Murphy-Dolan outfit, and the feud threatened to burst into flames at the slightest pretext. Both parties wanted contról of the Pecos River ranges. Into this melting-pot of hatred and treachery rode the indomitable Henry Brown, who cared not a tinker's cuss for whom he fought, just as long as he was paid regularly and plenty of excitement was furnished.

Scarcely had Brown become acquainted with the lie of the land when an excited cowboy asked him to join the Chisum faction.

'If he's paying high wages, tell your boss he has another gun-hand,' Henry informed the man. Henry, an expert with the rifle, was reluctant to apply for such a job and use that type of weapon. He had left his Sharps back in Kansas, and was prepared to rely on his expert handling of his six-guns.

The smouldering fire burst into flames with the foul murder of J. H. Tunstall as he made his way to Lincoln. Dick Brewer, fore-man of Tunstall's ranch, immediately contacted Tunstall's partner McSween, who went before Justice of the Peace John P. Wilson and had Brewer appointed a special constable. Now armed with legal authority, Brewer gathered a posse and set out to arrest the men responsible. In Brewer's party were Billy the Kid and Henry Brown. Morton and Baker, the two men they wanted, were located in a dugout and held the band at bay until their ammunition ran out. Constable Brewer told them they would not be harmed if they surrendered, but Billy the Kid, a close friend of Tunstall, killed both prisoners while on the way to Lincoln. McClosky, one of Brewer's men, attempted to save them, and was shot from his saddle by Henry Brown.

Henry Brown was also one of the posse which attempted to kill Buckshot Roberts. Roberts, however, killed Brewer and wounded another man in a fight at Blazer's Mill. Mortally wounded, the old Texan still managed to hold off his attackers and was left to die in peace.

Following the end of the Lincoln County war, Henry Brown and Billy the Kid refused to accept the amnesty offer of Territorial Governor Lew Wallace, both choosing to continue their lives of crime. All through the fight Henry Brown had worked hard to achieve notoriety, but his exploits were always overshadowed by those of Billy the Kid. Even though Henry had sided with the Kid in all his devilry, and had killed just as many men as Billy, he was over-looked while the Kid became nationally known as the number one badman of the wild and woolly West.

Henry Brown enjoyed being outside the law. He decided to break away from Billy the Kid and to make a name for himself. In many ways Brown and the Kid were similar. Both were fair-headed, had blue eyes, and were endowed with the same diabolical dispositions—blood-thirsty, treacherous, and homicidal. Brown was also said to be equal to the Kid on the draw, and just as deadly. So while Billy the Kid chose to stay in New Mexico, Henry Brown decided to seek adventure elsewhere. Brown's last association with the Kid was late in 1878, when they drove some stolen horses into Tascosa, in the Texas Panhandle. Brown did not return to New Mexico with Billy the Kid, but remained in the town to become, of all things, its first constable.

It was common practice in the old West to hire killers to keep other killers in line. Henry Brown was a good constable, and his New Mexico reputation had preceded him to Tascosa. He was so feared that no gunslinger would tackle him. It was not long before Henry became bored with the job, and left Texas for Fort Griffin. There he learned that the Cherokee Strip was soon to be opened to white settlers seeking homesteads, and also that Stoner's store, adjacent to Indian Territory, had become the meeting-place for all types of riff-raff and gunmen. Near Stoner's place a town had sprung up almost overnight, and it was named Caldwell. Gamblers, gunmen, and men and women of all creeds and professions flocked to the new Kansas town. They proceeded to make Caldwell the most evil, wild, and attractive town west of the mighty Mississippi.

Caldwell sounded just right to Henry Brown. He decided to make it his next stopping-place. Travellers whom he met upon the trail relayed to his eager ears the latest news of the town. He decided that Caldwell was the most lawless town then in the West. Killings were frequent, law-men were helpless, and anyone having the nerve to wear a badge was committing suicide. Good wages were offered deputies—with no takers!

Deputy Sheriff George S. Brown was the first lawman to be killed. George W. Flapp, his assistant, was made town marshal, but the nervous strain forced him to seek refuge in the whisky bottle. Before that he had tangled with a group of Texans, and in two days killed five men. Several days later he was riddled with buckshot from ambush.

Deputy Marshal Frank Hunt then took over. He lasted exactly one week, during which time he killed seven men. While attempting to make an arrest in the Texas House he was shot dead. Several more peace officers followed him. One was gunned down by the Jim Talbott gang, and another died on the floor of the Red Light Dance Hall on June 22, 1882.

When Henry Brown rode into Caldwell a certain B. O. (Bat) Carr was the marshal. Valuing his life, Carr had lined himself up with those who ruled the town, and had hired deputies to act as targets for those bent upon homicide.

On the trail Henry had made a decision. The excitement offered a peace officer in Caldwell appealed greatly to him, so he decided to seek out the marshal and apply for the vacancy of deputy marshal of Caldwell.

Brown rode up to the office of Mayor Hizzoner, halted his mount, and dropped stiffly from his saddle. Throwing off some of the trail dust, Henry walked up the steps leading to the porch. There he found an elderly man seated in a wide rocking-chair, nervously wringing his hands.

'Mayor Hizzoner?'

'Yes. What can I do for you, young man?'

'I hear you need a new deputy, and I'd like to have the job.'

'You! Why, you're not more than a boy—or, at least, not much more.' The mayor began to smile.

The deadly glint in Henry's cold blue eyes seemed to send him reeling back. Mayor Hizzoner then looked Henry over—closely. He had failed perhaps to see the two pearl-handled Colts draped on Brown's lean hips, or the .44 Winchester cradled in his arm, or the decided thrust of the young man's jaw. He failed to recognize in the applicant a full-grown, expert gunman, one who had sent a number of men to their graves, and not a punk show-off hoping to make a name for himself.

Hizzoner handed Henry Brown a five-pointed deputy's badge.

'Here, pin this on. You are now a deputy marshal of Caldwell, Kansas. Report to Bat Carr, he's the marshal. I hope you live until morning, and good luck.'

'Thanks,' said Henry as he walked away.

Pinning on the badge, he made his way to the Texas House Saloon. The bartender grinned as the new deputy pushed his way through the batwing doors.

'Hello, Marshal,' he said, 'going to be with us long?'

'That all depends. Where is Marshal Carr?'

'That's him sitting to the rear of the room. You'll always find a whisky bottle handy when he's around.'

As Henry turned to meet his new boss an instant buzzing went around the room. In a few minutes everyone there knew that the visitor was the new deputy, and they were already giving odds as to how long he would last.

'Your name Carr?' inquired Henry.

'Yes, why?'

'I'm your new deputy, for better or for worse,' Henry told him.

'Who in hell appointed you?'

'Mayor Hizzoner.'

'Hell, he's always going over my head! Oh, well, all right by me. You start on the night shift, around six.'

Henry executed a quick turnabout and left the saloon. He then obtained a quiet room and prepared for action. He cleaned and oiled his six-guns, got them ready for instant use by practising his quick draw before the mirror in his room. He then placed fresh cartridges in his guns and spent the few remaining hours in quiet, observant manœuvres. He did not advertise his intentions by presenting himself in the streets to attract attention, but confined his quest to learning the locations of all entrances and exits of the various saloons, honky-tonks, and gambling halls.

While Henry was making his plans, so were others. Sandy Jim, boss gunman and gambler, called some of his cronies together in the Golden Wedding Saloon. As the three men talked, their notched gun-butts displayed grim evidence of their prowess.

'We'll take care of him tonight when he passes the Golden Wedding,' grinned Sandy Jim.

As Deputy Marshal Henry Brown was a methodical person, it was exactly six o'clock when he stepped into the street. Down Main Street he walked, passing the red-light district, the blacksmith's shop, and Hubble's General Store. He glanced in at the Red Light Dance Hall, and saw that all was peaceful, with no trouble brewing. It seemed as though everyone was waiting for something to happen.

'What have they got in mind for me?' Henry wondered. He would soon know.

As he passed the Golden Wedding Saloon several shots sounded

127

from the bar-room. Shouts that might have been those of a drunken Texas cowboy rent the night air, then three more shots sounded. Henry recognized an old trick—he was being baited as the other deputies had. They wanted him to rush in to quiet a fake drunk and then they would gun him down.

Assuring himself that no one was watching, Henry turned from the front door, where he knew he was expected, and ran through an alleyway leading to the rear entrance. Like an Apache Indian, he entered the bar-room from the rear. Just as he had thought, all present were intently watching the front door, and none present became aware that the trick had backfired until they heard Henry command: 'Deputy Brown speaking. Put up your hands!'

The crowd turned, gaping with amazement. The two 'put-up' men went for their guns. They thought Henry must be crazy, for his six-guns were still in their holsters. Like streaks of lightning Henry's Colts leaped into his hands. When the firing stopped the two men lay dead on the floor. The fake drunk stood as though petrified. Henry walked up to the man and pistol-whipped him. Then turning to ringleader Sandy Jim, Brown said: 'I'll still be around if you want another try.'

Sandy Jim could hardly wait for the next day. He rushed to Marshal Carr's home and demanded that he get rid of Henry Brown at once.

'Who, me? Man, you're crazy,' said Carr. 'He'd never stand for it, especially not now.'

'You better do as I say, or you'll take the one-way trip to Boot Hill yourself.'

'All right, I'll try,' cringed the marshal.

Henry Brown was seated in the jail office, half asleep, when Marshal Carr stomped into the room. His courage bolstered with whisky, Carr blurted out: 'Brown, you're fired. Get your things and get out.'

Henry Brown rose slowly. 'You got it backwards, Marshal. You're the one who's fired.' He leaned over the desk and jerked off Carr's marshal's badge, at the same time placing his right hand on his pistol-butt. 'Any objections?' he added.

'No, none! I was going to leave this town soon, anyway,' stammered the ex-marshal.

Henry Brown

Having ousted his superior, Henry Brown presented himself before the city fathers and announced that he was appointing himself to fill the vacancy in the marshal's office, created by the sudden resignation of Bat Carr. Discretion proving the better part of valour, the city council to a man gave its consent.

Shortly after Henry's self-appointment to the marshal's job a minstrel show arrived in Caldwell. It was learned that the performers were scheduled to parade down Main Street, wearing high silk hats. Sandy Jim got the idea to use the hats as targets, with a money pool going to the man who shot off the most.

Mayor Hizzoner was frantic. He rushed to Marshal Brown and demanded that the affair be called off.

'I can handle this, Mayor, to everyone's good,' Brown assured him. 'Just be patient.'

The parade started the next morning. Drums boomed and several musical instruments in inexperienced hands made an attempt to play some national song. Marshal Brown managed to secure a position close to Sandy Jim. Sandy Jim fired at the first top hat that appeared and that piece of wearing apparel fell to the dusty street. Quick as a cat, Henry Brown drew his revolver and fired a slug close to Jim's new boots.

'What in hell's the idea, Brown?' demanded Sandy Jim.

'Dance!' cried Marshal Brown, and fired his gun again and again.

As Sandy Jim hopped about in the street Brown cried out: 'Call that dancing? Try running.' Again Brown's revolver roared, and Sandy Jim fell dead in the dust.

The dead man's astonished friends did not try to avenge Sandy's murder. 'He was resisting arrest,' was what Brown said.

About this time Marshal Brown sent a wire to a former friend of the Lincoln County war days. This character was Benjamin F. Wheeler, a tall, wavy-haired individual with a drooping moustache. His sad eyes and melancholy attitude masked his real homicidal nature. He was one of these gunmen who had no more compunction in shooting down a man than in brushing away a fly which annoyed him. He was as treacherous as a rattler, but never gave warning of attack.

Marshal Brown had put into force an anti-gun ordinance. All

weapons were supposed to be checked while a man was in town. Wheeler, a pawn in the hands of the shrewd Brown, always enforced this ordinance and killed several men in the process. In one instance Wheeler arrested a man named Morton Boyce. The prisoner was rude and insulting, especially to Marshal Brown. Soon after Wheeler told Brown about it, Boyce was found dead in the street. The marshal explained that he had shot the prisoner when he attempted to escape.

Caldwell was quiet and tamed by October. Time hung heavily upon Henry Brown's shoulders. Now he became surly and troublesome, no longer caring to enforce the law when it was not done at the point of a fast and exploding pistol. With his split personality, he was ready to join the opposite side if it provided danger and an opportunity for more killings.

In April 1884 Brown suggested to Ben Wheeler that they rob the bank at Medicine Lodge, Kansas.

'What for, Henry? We're sitting pretty good here.'

Brown hit Wheeler in a soft spot and ignored his question.

'There's a lot of money there, Ben, and I know we can use it. We can be back here in safety before anyone knows what happened.'

Henry Brown's jurisdiction ended at the town limits of Caldwell, but when word reached him that horse thieves were operating on the outskirts the marshal said he was going to look into the matter. It was the excuse he needed. Fully armed, he and Wheeler left Caldwell.

A few miles beyond Caldwell, either by appointment or by accident, Brown and Wheeler met Bill Smith and John Wesley.

The four gunmen rode into Medicine Lodge early on May 1. It was raining, and that seemed to please Henry. It would keep people indoors. In front of the bank Brown told Smith to hold the horses in readiness while he, Wheeler, and Wesley went inside. Brown drew his pearl-handled pistols and pushed through the bank door, closely followed by his two cronies, guns also drawn.

'Hello, Mr. Brown,' greeted Mr. Wiley Payne, the bank president.

'This is a hold-up, Payne,' replied Brown. 'Put up your hands.'

Wheeler covered the cashier, George Geppert, and kept an eye on the front door at the same time.

Payne was no coward. He tried to grab a pistol in the desk drawer. Brown fired, and the bullet dropped Payne to the floor. Ben

Wheeler lost his head and fired at the cashier. Geppert, dying, staggered to the vault door and twisted the lock dial.

Just as Northfield, Minnesota, was the Waterloo of the James-Younger gang, so Medicine Lodge, Kansas, was the end of the trail for the Henry Brown bunch. Empty-handed, the three killers fled. Bill Smith still held the horses, but a body of men, firing as they came, rushed towards the outlaws. Brown grabbed his Winchester and drove them back with five fast-fired shots.

Into the Gypsum Hills rode the four outlaws, closely pursued by a posse led by Marshal Barney O'Connor of Medicine Lodge. This was strange country to the outlaws. What looked like a canyon offering an avenue of escape ended in high cliffs, impassable to man or beast.

The four wanted men leaped from their mounts and fortified themselves behind large boulders. Wesley and Wheeler whimpered, but Brown and Smith were made of sterner stuff.

'We'll fight our way out,' said Brown.

But it was a hopeless fight. By noon most of their ammunition had been used and the determined posse was closing in.

They all agreed to call it quits, so Brown tied a wet handkerchief to the barrel of his Winchester and waved it slowly in the air.

The prisoners were returned to Medicine Lodge and secured in a wooden shack which served as the jail. The bank president was still alive at the time the outlaws were captured.

A lynch mob circled the crude and weakly built jail. The county attorney wanted statements from the prisoners, so he was allowed to enter the building and talk with them.

'Payne still lives,' he said, 'but if he dies I'm afraid no one will be able to stop that mob.'

The mob grew larger as the night lengthened. Sometime during the first hours of darkness Payne passed away. Four hangman's nooses were tied as the crowd converged upon the jail. The county sheriff and his men gathered before the door, but their resistance would be weak at best. The prisoners managed to get their shackles off about the same time two huge men crashed in the jail door.

'Fight, Ben!' cried Henry Brown.

Ben Wheeler knocked aside the first of the men who tried to enter the jail. Brown rushed through the opening and dashed into the street. He had gone about a block when he fell dead with two loads of buckshot in his back.

Wheeler was wounded from the blast of a .45 and managed to run several hundred yards before he was recaptured. Wesley and Smith made little effort to escape.

The mob dragged the prisoners to the bottomlands near Medicine Lodge. Three ropes were thrown over a limb of an oak-tree. Wesley and Wheeler pleaded for mercy. The plucky Smith merely said: 'Let's get it over with.'

For the record, the coroner held a hearing the next day. He declared that Henry Brown, Benjamin Wheeler, William Smith, and John Wesley had met their deaths at the hands of persons unknown.

As in the case of other noted gunmen, the word got out that Henry Brown was not killed that day in 1884; that someone else was responsible for the attempted bank robbery and the murders at Medicine Lodge.

Lucius Dills, long-time resident in Roswell, stated that Henry Brown went to Tascosa, Texas, after that date, where he served as a deputy sheriff under Sheriff C. B. Willingham. Later, he claimed, Brown served as a deputy sheriff under Sheriff Higgins of Chaves County, New Mexico. After his service with Sheriff Higgins this particular Brown faded into obscurity and was never heard of again. But no doubt this was another Henry Brown. Had it been *the* Henry Brown he never would have gone willingly into obscurity.

On the other side of the ledger we have an item which appeared on May 17, 1884, in the Lincoln County *Leader*:

Readers of the daily papers are familiar with the facts of the attempted bank robbery at Medicine Lodge, Kansas, and the killing of the president and cashier of the institution by four men whose names were Henry N. Brown, Marshal of Caldwell, Kansas, Ben Wheeler, his assistant, W. Smith, and a man by the name of Wesley, both cowboys. The citizens gave pursuit, and the quartette of robbers were caught and lynched. The man Brown had been married but six weeks, and was a member of Billy the Kid's gang in the Lincoln County war. Better for the world that he has gone.

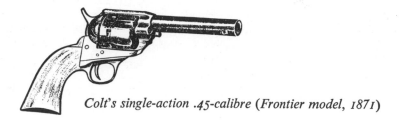

Colt's single-action .45-calibre (Frontier model, 1871)

7 Ben Thompson

IN THE frontier town of Austin, Texas, in the year 1856, a thirteen-year-old printer's apprentice was brought to trial for shooting mustard seed into the buttocks of a playmate. His English parents engaged a capable attorney, who presented the defence that the boy had shot on a dare, and that he showed sympathy with the victim's pain while the shot was being removed from the flesh. The jury recommended clemency, the judge delayed sentence, and Governor H. R. Runnels issued a pardon.

This is the first recorded incident in the life of Ben Thompson, whose career from then on gurgles like a blood-bath. There was almost no extensive period during his forty-one years on earth when he was not guilty of shooting some man, and almost always he was under a charge of murder. But outwardly he showed such deference to the letter of the law and to enforcement officers that he almost always won acquittal. His faith in his own righteousness gave him a plausibility which smoothed the way for him on many occasions.

Thompson was a stout five foot nine. He had a swarthy complexion, black hair, and blue eyes. He possessed indomitable energy and was quick in all his motions. His mother and his wife and his son and daughter—possibly also his father, who was either lost at sea or else deserted the family on a trip to England—thought of him as the champion of underdogs and revered him for his generosity, though even they probably deplored his addiction to gambling.

Thompson as a youth went to New Orleans for adventure. But there he encountered such difficulty in making his way that he decided to book passage for San Francisco. After paying all the money he had for a berth, he reached the dock only to learn that the ship had sailed earlier than scheduled, leaving him penniless.

He thought he might be able to get a job in a printer's if he went back to the town. On a bus he saw a Frenchman offering unwelcome attentions to a young woman, and he affected a sudden chivalry. By accosting the Frenchman he became involved in a duel, and later killed him. As a result, he had to hide out in the Sicilian quarter, where hot tempers and murder were condoned. While a reward was offered for his apprehension, his new friends, defiant of any civic law, helped him escape across the river. He stole a mule, and rode back home to Austin.

Thompson resumed setting type, but he had by now acquired expensive tastes. Therefore he supplemented his earnings by the new method he had learned in New Orleans. He played faro, monte, roulette, rouge et noir, Boston, seven-up, euchre, draw poker, or any other of the gambling games which were then the rage. Before long he took a job as a monte dealer, and from then on he always 'relied upon his skill as applied to the laws of luck and chance'.

At the outbreak of the Civil War Thompson enlisted in Colonel John R. Taylor's regiment, and was on duty at Fort Clark, New Mexico. In a quarrel he shot and killed the mess sergeant and then attacked a lieutenant who had tried to interfere. The captain of the company put him under arrest, and in the guardhouse he was chained to the floor, flat on his back, for more than a month, without trial or court-martial.

Inducing a friend to supply him with matches, Thompson contrived to set the guardhouse on fire because he preferred death to further suffering. He was on the verge of suffocation when rescuers arrived to loosen his chains and carry him to safety.

The friend who had brought him the matches was about that time taken ill with what appeared to be smallpox, and Thompson was the only one who volunteered to nurse him. It turned out that the patient had merely a case of chicken-pox, but Thompson and he made use of the camp scare by escaping. They filled in the last twelve months of their enlistment at another Army post two hundred miles away.

At the time of Thompson's discharge the war was still in progress. He re-enlisted with a company on the march to Galveston for active service. During a stop-over at San Antonio, the soldiers elected him to sneak out at night for a supply of whisky. The sentry gave the alarm. In order to avoid pursuit Thompson had to turn along a paved section of road. His horse slipped and fell upon him, crushing his leg. He was caught and sent to the prison hospital for six weeks. In the meantime his regiment had moved on, so, without permission from the medical officers, he followed on crutches. He overtook the regiment in camp on the St. Bernard, and found that his best friend, Phil Coe, was under arrest but not under guard because he had given his parole. Phil was a civilian who had been acting as an officer without authority, and he had refused to enlist as a private.

Thompson and Coe slipped off one night to get some whisky and were carried back drunk. Because Thompson was still using crutches he was kept to the rear, among the sick. Coe was ordered to be conscripted, but he fled to Mexico, and stayed there until the close of the war. Thompson afterwards claimed that, although he had to move on crutches, he had participated in the capture of the *Harriet Lane* and the destruction of other Union vessels at Galveston.

However that may be, he quarrelled with another sergeant, beating him with his crutch. There might have been another murder on his record if the crutch had not broken after the first few blows. He was placed in the guardhouse, but two days later the whole command was ordered to Louisiana, and his refraction of rules was forgotten.

The regiment routed Pyron's opposition at La Fourche—and Thompson and his younger brother Billy found themselves to be the only living among the battlefield's dead.

Ben was in great pain because of his unhealed leg injury, and when he and Billy finally located the remainder of their company he was furloughed indefinitely. After a period of convalescence he obtained for both himself and Billy a transfer to the regiment of Colonel John S. Ford, Old Rip of Comanche battle fame. They joined him at Eagle Pass, for patrol duty along the eastern bank of the Rio Grande.

Billy had seventy dollars, which he allowed his older brother to use as a start in a monte game. Ben lost all the money, as well as his spurs and his hat, but he retained his six-shooter. As he said later: 'When that hatless, barefooted, one-gallus thing called luck frowns, a man sins against good gambling if he don't quit.'

In disgust over his hard luck, Thompson quarrelled with both soldiers and officers who had won, and finally he decided to go to a little Mexican village across the Border from Laredo, for a really good game. During the first night his winnings at monte were over twelve hundred dollars. This increased his daring, and, against his better judgment, he opened his game to Mexicans who, he knew, were crafty and experienced gamblers. After playing for many hours, and suspecting that the losers would soon be in a fighting mood, he signalled Billy to go and get his pistol. But the trouble broke out before Billy had returned, because it became apparent that Thompson meant to close the game while he was in possession of all the money as well as all the six-shooters of the other players.

There was considerable shooting when the two candles were extinguished, but Thompson and Billy were safe outside as the smoke cleared. They eluded the troops that galloped up to investigate the noise. It was, however, important that Thompson should not be seen in the neighbourhood. With great difficulty he managed to float himself across the river on an improvised raft. On his way to the home of a Mr. Riddle he had to pass along streets where Mexicans slept in the open. Watchdogs attacked him, one after another, and his flesh was torn in many parts of his legs and buttocks. He was bloody from the waist down and in great pain when he reached Mr. Riddle's house, but there his wounds were washed with ammonia and he was allowed to sleep.

The next morning Thompson learned that the Mexican gamblers knew where he was staying. Evidently the savage dogs had marked his trail, though none of the Mexican owners of the dogs had chosen to wake up long enough to call off the animals. Before setting out again, Thompson sent a friend to ask Captain Carrington to ride with his men to a certain point on the river bank, so that when Thompson crossed he could be met by United States troops for his protection. Captain Carrington arrived exactly when needed, while Mexican troops watched, cheated of their quarry by only a few minutes.

136

However, Captain Carrington insisted that if Thompson were on the camp grounds when the Mexican officials requested that he be turned over, their request would be gratified. Thompson thereupon took several friends down the road along which they expected the Mexicans to pass, determined to kill as many of them as possible. But Captain Carrington, hearing of this plot, sent a messager to notify the Mexicans, who avoided the ambush.

Thompson joined Captain William Armstrong's company, but was not encouraged to stay, in view of the Mexican demand for his head. Therefore at three o'clock in the morning he hurried to join Captain Robert Gardner, who was in charge of a train of artillery. After further suffering from the dog-bites, the fugitive finally caught up with Captain Gardner, who set up cannon and prepared to fight the Mexicans rather than surrender Thompson.

Thompson arrived safely in Austin some time later and rested for a while with his family.

Colonel Ford detailed Thompson to raise a company and to join the regiment of Colonel Beard for operations against the Indians in the north-west. He started to sign up recruits, but the members of the home guard resented this. In a street brawl Thompson killed several of these local opponents. There was danger that a mob might storm his house during the night, so he stayed elsewhere until the following day. Then he refused to surrender to arrest, but declared he was willing to stand trial if he were left free on his own recognizance until the trial was called. It was long delayed, and when it finally opened the jury acquitted him without leaving the box.

Thompson succeeded in raising a company of volunteers and joined Beard's regiment near the city of Waco, but by then the Indians had quieted down. Very soon the collapse of the Confederacy changed the situation, and thousands of disbanded soldiers flooded the state, desperate, defeated, and impoverished.

Early in June 1865 Colonel Badger of the First Louisiana Cavalry arrived in Austin and issued an order for Thompson's arrest without making any specific charge. Thompson was placed in the Travis County jail and kept chained to the wall. But he made friends with his guards and planned an escape with them to Mexico, where they hoped to enter the service of the Emperor Maximilian.

Before long Thompson was in Mexico, marching into battle and receiving promotion for his bravery under fire. He was attached to a company which was besieged by a weak force, and frequently he broke through the lines with his men. On one occasion he intercepted a supply train and killed the soldiers in charge of it, commandeering the animals and the cargo.

Of course Thompson found, as usual, an opportunity to gamble, and his pistol remained his constant companion. After one long game there was a gunfight that drew the police. He was arrested and marched through the Mexican streets towards the city jail. But he was rescued by some Americans, and he killed a number of Mexican policemen while escaping. When the general under whom Thompson was serving asked for an explanation, he closed the interview by saying: 'Thompson, see that you don't let it happen again.' No reference was made to the murders.

In battle the next day, out of fourteen hundred men on Thompson's side eleven hundred were killed. Thompson had gone into the fight with fifty-eight men. At the close he had only seventeen left, eight of them seriously injured.

Perhaps looking for consolation, he appeared at a gambling house but lost heavily and, disgruntled, went on to a dance-hall. There between dances he had a fight with a Mexican whom he left dead on the floor before fleeing in the dark.

Once again Thompson had to explain to his general, who sighed and said: 'Never mind. We shall soon be far from here.'

At four o'clock the next morning the regiment marched to help Maximilian. They covered four hundred miles in ninety-six hours and entered Queretaro on the fourth night shortly after midnight. Accompanying his general, Thompson had audience with the Emperor, and was moved by his great dignity even in this hour of defeat.

At the close of the royal interview, the flag of Juarez was brought in with a demand for unconditional surrender. The Emperor surely thought he would be given time to reply, but an immediate assault was begun. He and his generals were surrounded and taken captive.

Thompson escaped from Queretaro and overtook a rider on a fresh mount, whom he forced to trade horses with him. He rode furiously over two hundred and eighty miles· towards Vera Cruz, where he knew he could join the French commander, Bazaine. He told himself that now, with the war over, he would travel to the Pacific coast as quickly as possible, to try his luck in the goldfields of California.

But he was struck down by yellow fever, and for many months was nursed by Sisters of Charity. While he was convalescing a stray New York newspaper fell into his hands, and he read that civil government had been established in Texas under Governor J. W. Throckmorton. He was homesick, and took the first occasion to return to Austin. However, on arriving he discovered that the military still had plenty of power in the region, and that was not good news for him.

Because there were several indictments still pending against him in Austin, Thompson remained on the outskirts of the town at the home of a relative. But his handsome horse with its silver-mounted saddle, whose housings were of long black hair plaited into highly dressed leather, challenged the attention of the soldiers camped north of the capital. They learned the name of its owner and decided at their own discretion to arrest Thompson. However, the gambler suspected their plan when he saw a soldier guarding his horse, which he had sent for shoeing.

He approached the horse. He was dressed like a young hidalgo, in blue trousers, with silver cords down the seams, embroidered buckskin jacket, a wide stiff-brimmed, low-crowned hat with a golden snake coiled around it as a band. About his waist he wore a red sash to cover his pistol. While he took hold of his horse's bridle rein with his left hand he grasped his pistol with his right.

The soldier was greatly surprised to be ordered to hand over his pistol, but he did so and stepped back when he found the muzzle of Thompson's gun at his nose. Thompson leaped into the saddle and rode off to the Cedar Mountains. A squad of troops almost captured him when his horse stumbled and fell, but he got away without being hit. He led his injured horse into a thicket and hid quietly until his pursuers were out of earshot.

After this incident Thompson consulted his attorneys and urged them to bring him to trial so that his innocence could be established, for he claimed that he had never killed except in self-defence. At the trial he was acquitted of all charges brought against him.

Thompson next turned to his favourite vocation, gambling, in the city of Bryan, a thriving town on the Houston and Texas Central Railway. A gigantic man named Big King, proprietor of the Blue Wing Saloon, one night lost heavily to him, but still did not want to quit. He offered to bet his saloon if Thompson would continue after daylight. Thompson was practically worn out, but agreed, and the two men played through that day and another night without rest. By daylight of the following day Big King had lost the Blue Wing and Thompson was installed as proprietor. He ordered champagne and treated all the men in the house.

He had the back room fitted up for gambling. A few nights later Thompson returned in time to find his dealer being threatened by some gamblers who had lost heavily. Practically everything in the Blue Wing was broken in the fight that ensued.

Thompson's brother Billy, during an argument in a house of prostitution, killed an Army sergeant and went into hiding. Thompson was not able to go to his brother because he was constantly shadowed, but he managed to send provisions. As a rule, to prevent the Army from discovering the boy's whereabouts, Thompson sent a messenger in the wrong direction with a note urging Billy to make a certain journey. This usually misled the patrol. But on one occasion the troops did learn where Billy was. Learning this, Thompson armed himself and rode swiftly to his brother, gave him his horse and directed him to a new shelter, then returned to the city by a roundabout route.

The sheriff and a big posse later found out where Billy was hiding while Thompson was in the same house with him. They surrounded the house and attacked at about one o'clock at night. They made a tremendous noise in trying to get through the bushes and vines and briars and prickly pears. Ben and Billy were both out of the house and gone long before the posse had reached the front door. Eighteen days later Billy arrived safely in the Indian Nations.

Once Thompson found himself in danger of using his pistol on a man who repeatedly annoyed him. For his own safety's sake he appealed to a magistrate for help, but was refused. The next time the man annoyed him Thompson shot him, inflicting a flesh wound that was not fatal. The gunman then returned to the magistrate and asked to be put under bond to appear to face an indictment on this count. The magistrate again refused. Presently Thompson heard that this same magistrate was preparing a warrant for his arrest by a military commission. Incensed, he again called at the magistrate's office.

'A short time ago,' said Thompson, 'you couldn't draw up a warrant because you didn't know how, and now you are able to prepare this difficult document!'

He lost his temper and forced the magistrate to get out of his own office, saying: 'If I ever see you playing officer again I'll kill you, if I hang for it.'

The magistrate dodged away through an alley. In less than half an hour Ben Thompson was in the hands of the military, heavily ironed and enclosed in the 'bull pen'. This was a small space securely surrounded with broad walls upon which sentries walked with loaded rifles. When two drunken soldiers attacked another inmate Thompson, in a spirit of chivalry, hit one of them with his closed knife, driving it through the man's eyeball.

For this he was put in double irons and chains, and fastened to the ground so that he could not move from side to side nor lift his arms or legs. Thus he lay every night for nearly a month. The irons ate into his flesh, and because he endured this affliction courageously several of the guards expressed their sympathy—though they did not dare to show him any favours.

Thompson was finally arraigned, and the trial lasted for five weeks, costing the Government 15,000 dollars. Each day of the trial Thompson was forced to walk to it, a distance of over one mile, carrying his fetters. The flesh of his ankles became lacerated, and his socks were saturated with blood.

When sentence was read Thompson and another prisoner, both emaciated by their prison treatment, were refused permission to see their families. They were escorted by two hundred and twelve men to the Huntsville penitentiary. Thompson was kept in solitary confinement until his wounds were sufficiently healed to permit him to do hard labour. After a couple of months he was assigned to the hair department, and became an expert in plaiting, twisting, and weaving hair into fashionable articles. He remained there for two years—until the military was transferred from this section of the country, at which time he was summarily dismissed.

Thompson returned to his family in Austin and also to gambling, for that was now his only means of earning a livelihood. When he had accumulated funds to enable him to travel he moved to Abilene, where Texas drovers congregated regularly and where he felt he would be operating among friends. After a long spell of bad luck he was at last able to quit with 2,583 dollars in his pockets.

Just at this time Thompson's old friend Phil Coe arrived in Abilene with several thousand dollars of his own. Together they opened a saloon, making it the town's headquarters for gambling, and they prospered. Wild Bill Hickok became marshal, drawing fifty per cent of all fines collected and also receiving regular cuts of profits from various gamblers. Thompson and Phil Coe refused to pay such protection money, and knew they had to be prepared for trouble.

Thompson sent for his wife and children now that he had enough money to give them a comfortable home, and on the first day of their reunion he took them on a buggy ride to show them the surrounding country. As they drove over an unexpected hole in the roadway the buggy was overturned, and they were all injured. Ben's leg was broken, his little boy's foot was crushed, and his wife's arms were shattered. They were picked up by strangers and carried to the Lindell Hotel in Kansas City, where they had to undergo medical treatment for three months. Thompson wrote Phil Coe about his difficulties, and Phil Coe telegraphed him three thousand dollars. When they were able to travel the whole Thompson family set out for Austin, knowing that Thompson's mother would nurse them.

They were travelling by easy stages when they were overtaken by a party carrying a casket, and for the first time Thompson learned that Wild Bill Hickok had shot his best friend, Phil Coe, and had closed the prosperous saloon which he and Phil Coe had been operating. Thompson had thus lost everything.

It was a long time before he recovered his health. Then he went to Ellsworth, Kansas, where his brother Billy was one of the men delivering cattle on the hoof to the rail terminus. Together they collected enough money to set up gambling rooms.

During a fight with a man named Martin, who had refused to share his winnings, the whole town was aroused by Thompson's shooting in the street. Sheriff Whitney, a friend of Thompson, was anxious to avoid bloodshed, so he persuaded Thompson and Billy to go with him to the Grand Central Hotel. On the way there was another mêlée, and Billy, attempting to shoot a man who was aiming at Thompson, shot Sheriff Whitney. Thompson got his brother on to a fleet mount with some money and told him to ride for his life, but the boy was not exactly aware of his danger.

'I made up my mind,' said Thompson later, 'that if the mob should get hold of Billy I'd empty my gun and pistol into its ranks.'

Billy got away, and Thompson saw a group of men with drawn guns approaching him. To his surprise they did not see where he was leaning against a post, but marched beyond him, calling out to others: 'Where are those murderers, the Thompsons?'

Thompson was within ten feet of them, so he drew a bead on them and said quietly: 'The man who moves I shall kill. Lay down your arms.'

He held them at bay until Mayor Miller appeared, and then Thompson offered to surrender if the mayor would first disarm the hostile men. This was done, and Thompson went with the mayor to his office. Since it was too late in the day for a trial, the mayor asked some residents to post a 10,000-dollar bond for Thompson, who was then released.

Thompson spent the evening at the theatre, seeing *She Stoops to Conquer*, and during the performance a friend tapped his shoulder and whispered: 'Billy's back in town.'

Thompson knew that regular and special law enforcement officers were scouring the country for his brother at that very moment, and he was shocked to hear of the boy's return. He found him in a small upstairs room, and Billy made him see his reason.

'The country for a long distance is full of officers,' Billy explained, 'and the authorities have telegraphed in all directions. It would be foolish for me to try to pass out of this locality now.'

Thompson helped his brother disguise himself by cutting his long hair and then colouring his whole body, even between the toes, to make him look like a Mexican. He painted his teeth yellow to resemble the stain of tobacco juice. In Mexican boots and a cap and black clothes with a secondhand blue Army blouse, Billy was soon ready to drive stock, as he had been doing before. He was even able to speak Spanish, so he continued at his job until he had a chance to leave for a safer region.

When Thompson appeared for his trial there were no witnesses against him, and the case was dismissed. Within a week he had left for Kansas City, from where he later went to St. Louis, then by boat to New Orleans, and so back home to Austin.

About this time the competition between the Atchison, Topeka, and Santa Fe Railroad and the Denver and Rio Grande had reached a danger point. The Atchison engaged Thompson for a bonus of five thousand dollars to protect their roundhouse until they should have time to appeal to the law. With a carefully worded agreement, to the effect that Thompson would be required to fight only against an unauthorized body of men if they should attack the roundhouse, the deal was concluded. Thompson took charge and barricaded the place.

The Denver and Rio Grande officials offered him twenty-five thousand dollars if he would surrender the roundhouse to them, but he replied: 'I will die here unless the law relieves me.' This of course was his own version of the episode, though there were currently other versions.

When Thompson was relieved by law enforcement officers he returned home by way of St. Louis, this time with money for his family. He established a gambling house in the second story of a downtown building, but the work made him lose sleep. He became pale and was, in fact, not in his usual robust health. Some strangers who mistook him for a weakling once heckled him, and he let them continue with their insulting remarks out of curiosity. Suddenly he revealed his true identity and, too late, they tried to retreat. In their flight one of them caught two of Thompson's bullets.

Again he submitted to arrest and was bonded. Within the next two months he was indicted, tried, and acquitted of assault with intent to kill. He always had very persuasive lawyers to defend him, and his constant care to co-operate with officers won their co-operation in return.

One evening Thompson left his gambling rooms in the charge of his partner, Loraine. But he felt he had several grievances against Loraine. These developed greater proportions as he steadily drank champagne at dinner with his friend Bill Johnson. At length, in a terribly belligerent mood, he insisted on going back to have it out with Loraine. Bill Johnson went along, hoping to prevent trouble, and with this end in view he even searched Thompson and satisfied himself that the gambler was unarmed.

However, Thompson had secreted a pistol in his clothes, and he drew it out at the least expected moment. He shot the pile of chips and the dealer's box and the chandelier.

'Loraine,' he said, 'you can buy another set of tools and charge them to me. I don't like the ones you had.'

The police whistle sounded, and Bill Johnson forced Thompson out the back door. They went down to the Iron-Front Saloon, where the keno rooms were being operated by a man named Simon. Thompson began shooting into the cylinder-shaped box that works on its axis, holding the balls with which the game is played. At the first sound of shooting all the players and dealers and waiters, and indeed everyone else attached to the establishment, left through the doors and windows and up the stairs and over the roofs of neighbouring houses. Again the police congregated, but Thompson was no longer there.

Bill Johnson continued to remonstrate with him, but without any effect on Thompson, who by this time had worked up such momentum that nothing could stop him. He led the way to the First Ward and shot out the street lights and the lamps which marked the houses of prostitution. The police rushed towards the shooting, but by the time they arrived there was shooting in another district. Thompson led them on a wild chase through dark streets.

Usually, however, Ben Thompson was in a more sober mood. To the surprise of many citizens, he actually became a candidate for the office of marshal in Austin. The incumbent won the election, but 744 men voted for Thompson in spite of his unsavoury reputation. After this defeat he went to Colorado and New Mexico for several months.

As soon as he had returned and started another gambling room, he met new trouble. He and several cronies late one night crossed the street to attend the Variety Theatre, and Thompson roared with laughter when he saw one young man set off some firecrackers. Of course, anything that sounded like firearms started confusion in the audience. Mark Wilson, the stout, red-faced, impulsive proprietor, who was a deputy sheriff especially so that he could keep order at the theatre, rushed from behind the scenes to find out what was going on.

A wag who had some lampblack leaned up to the stage and stroked Wilson's face with it, drawing a laugh from the audience.

Wilson cried: 'Officer, arrest that man!' pointing to the man with the lampblack.

Thompson stood up at his table and called: 'Officer, I'll be responsible for the prisoner. He was only trying to have a little fun and meant no harm. I'll have him at the mayor's office tomorrow morning. Don't lock him up for a harmless joke.'

'Who is running this house—you or me?' cried Wilson, turning on Thompson in fury.

Thompson fingered his gun, a gesture which usually induced everybody present to let him lead the discussion his own way. But in this case Wilson was not intimidated, being an officer of the law in his own right and in his own premises.

'You're probably the one who instigated this disorderly conduct in the first place,' he snapped.

It was later Thompson's claim that when he denied this Wilson accused him of lying. At any rate, Thompson slapped Wilson's face.

Wilson chose not to reply in kind, but instead he walked down the aisle towards the bar where his firearms were hung. When he had a double-barrelled shotgun in his hands he called out loudly: 'Clear the way!' He cocked the gun and brought it to bear in the direction of Thompson.

Members of the audience darted, dodged, squatted, crawled, did everything to get out of the way. As soon as the aisle was clear the shooting began. Thompson claimed that Wilson fired first and tore a hole in his clothes above the hip, that only when Wilson was about to fire the second time did he himself fire. Thompson's first shot at Wilson crippled him, and then he shot him several times after he had fallen. When Thompson saw the bartender raising a gun he shot at him too. The bartender dodged behind the bar, but the shot went through the woodwork and broke his lower jaw. He died several weeks later.

Completely satisfied with his success over the impudent Wilson, Thompson immediately walked over to the sheriff's office and surrendered.

'Looks to me as though a mob is forming to attack you,' said the sheriff.

Thompson answered: 'Don't endanger yourself for my sake, Sheriff. Prepare me with a few good pistols, and I'll defend myself.' This time, however, the law was permitted to take its course. At the preliminary trial the judge committed Thompson to jail without bail. On a writ of *habeas corpus* the prisoner was taken to Galveston, where the Court of Appeals was in session, and he was released on a 5,000-dollar bond. When an indictment had been prepared in Travis County, he was tried, and the jury, after deliberating for only a few minutes, returned with a verdict of 'not guilty'.

Because the Indians were becoming troublesome again, Thompson joined the Rangers, commanded by Captain Ed Burleson, son of the honoured General Burleson who had repelled the redskins a generation earlier. The company left for the headwaters of the Brazos River to drive the Indians from the border, but they were drawn farther and farther into the desert as the Indians retreated. Water was found only at great intervals and often was unfit to drink until it was filtered through sand to eliminate salt and other minerals. By the time the Rangers had kept up their pursuit as far as the Pecos and Canadian rivers, their horses had been galloping for forty days and the riders themselves were in need of rest. Consequently, Captain Burleson camped for ten days north of the Concho River and south of the Red Fork of the Colorado. At this place the water was good, the grass fine, and buffalo and elk abundant.

Of course Thompson had his monte cards along. As counters the men used pieces of copper ore which they found lying about on the ground. It was a profitable time of 'rest' for the gambler.

After camp had been broken and the march resumed Captain Burleson detailed Thompson to scout ahead to make sure that no Indians were over the horizon. Thompson chose Buckskin Sam to ride with him, and they climbed a hill from which they could see for considerable distances in several directions.

As Thompson described it:

The sun, descending through what seemed to be a yellowish haze, was red as blood, the air as still as death, save a dull, heavy, regular, distant sound. The earth trembled beneath us, the red, angry, avenging sun, the oppressive silence broken only by the strange sound. The quaking, shaking earth impressed me with an awful fear.

147

Thompson put spurs to his horse and rode rapidly to the crest of the next hill. There he saw, coming up the slope towards him, thousands of buffalo, making a noise like thunder. They were rushing madly ahead. But then he discovered that in the midst of the wild herd eighty or a hundred Comanches were riding. He could see their long black hair floating in the wind, their eagle-feather adornments waving from side to side as they swayed on their fast-moving horses. Their faces were disfigured with red and black war-paint. Their lances were held in one hand, and their bows and quivers full of arrows were slung across their shoulders.

Thompson and Buckskin Sam prepared to fly back to their detachment, but it seemed important to do something to slow down the redskins before they could advance much farther. In spite of the danger they were in, the two scouts checked their horses long enough to take aim and shoot. The two leaders of the Indians fell. While Thompson and Buckskin Sam were dashing off to save their lives, they once more checked their horses and fired. They were so well satisfied with the result of these tactics that they risked stopping and shooting even for a third time. Taking their courage in their hands when the whole herd with the Indian war-party seemed about to swoop down on them, they halted, took aim, and fired.

This time Thompson's horse was killed, and he rolled over the ground while a flight of arrows went over his head. Buckskin Sam flung himself to the ground and joined Thompson behind the prostrate horse, which they used as a barricade while they continued to shoot.

Fortunately for them, Captain Burleson on the other side of the rise had heard the shooting and had arrived with his entire con-tingent. The Rangers drove the confused Comanches back over the hill once more—and Thompson never did explain what happened to the herd of maddened buffalo.

Thompson returned to Austin with this story and several others, to enhance his pose of hero. Another election was in the offing, and once more he became a candidate. This time he won the marshalship. He enjoyed parading in his uniform and took pride in keeping the lawless element out of the city. At every hour of the day and night he was on duty, and it is claimed that during his period in office there was not a murder nor an assault with intent to kill within the limits of the city. Moreover, not a burglary or theft was committed but what the criminal was promptly brought to trial and punished.

In 1880 Thompson engaged one of his attorneys, William M. Walton, to write his life-story. He felt this was called for because his belief in himself as a public figure had reached incredible dimensions. Besides, he was so powerful that everyone with whom he came in contact cheerfully verified his own opinion of himself. Dutifully, Walton wrote a paean of praise—but the tone of the last part of this book changed when Thompson was no longer able to supervise its preparation. Only after Thompson's death did Walton dare to admit that the gambler had sometimes used intoxicating liquor to excess, or even that at times he had acted unreasonably.

Friends had invited Thompson's little daughter and son to visit them in San Antonio, and the children had been begging their father to take them. At last he had time to do so, and after many preparations they left for the short ride by rail. On arrival in San Antonio Thompson telegraphed his wife: ARRIVED SAFE—ALL WELL.—CHILDREN HAPPY—GOD BLESS YOU.

The children were handed over to the womenfolk, and the menfolk indulged in a social glass or two. During the confidences exchanged somebody said that in San Antonio there were some men, such as Jack Harris, who wanted to see Thompson assassinated.

Jack Harris was at the time conducting a gambling house in San Antonio, but he had once been a friend of Thompson. They had marched side by side in the Army and had slept under a single blanket on the ground. But in the intervening years Jack Harris had forgotten the old friendship and had developed an enmity towards the more famous gambler. There is no record of the reason for this change on his part.

While in San Antonio on this visit with his children, Thompson stopped at Jack Harris's place, and was betting at the table where Joe Foster was the dealer. Thompson's wide experience with cards made it possible for him to detect that things were not exactly right. He therefore changed his tactics and played so recklessly that the dealer could not keep up with his turns in the way he had started out to do at the beginning of the game. As a result, although Thompson had at first lost heavily, now he won all his losses back, to Foster's consternation.

When Thompson rose to leave the table with his winnings, he loudly denounced Foster as a swindler, and Foster reached for his pistol. But Thompson had his own pistol at Foster's face instantly.

'Any movement on your part is death,' he said carefully.

Foster remained rigid until Thompson, his pistol still pointing at him, had backed away and gone into the street.

When Harris, the owner of the place, heard this story, he naturally sided with Foster and said: 'Oh, the time will come when we'll get Thompson in a tight spot. Just wait.'

Thompson took his children back home, but he returned to San Antonio on an excursion to Laredo with the members of the Legislature and city officials. During their stop in San Antonio Thompson was told that Harris was in the street with a double-barrelled gun, avowing his intention of shooting him on sight.

When the two men met Thompson called out: 'Hello, Jack! Is it true you've been looking for me?'

'No,' said Harris, 'but if you come to my place I'll make you wish you hadn't.'

Thompson retorted: 'Go and get your gang and arm them, and meet me out at the Main Plaza. Come out and fight like men.'

Harris ignored this challenge, but at a number of places he talked freely about what he thought of Thompson. Gossip reached Thompson, of course, and he was informed that Harris had been threatening to kill him. This did nothing to calm him.

Harris was running the Vaudeville Variety Theatre. It was his habit to go home at four o'clock in the afternoon, then return at eleven o'clock in the evening after the theatre money had been collected. The ticket office was on the same floor as the bar, with swinging doors between the two, and he kept a double-barrelled shotgun in the office.

Thompson with a friend entered the bar and ordered drinks. He said to the bartender: 'Where's that shotgun brigade that's on the hunt for me?'

'Never heard of it,' said the bartender tactfully.

Later it was reported that Thompson next said: 'You tell Joe Foster he's a thief, and tell Jack Harris he's living off the labours of those poor variety women,' but this was hardly in line with Thompson's jovial mood. He usually kept his comments for strategic moments.

Thompson and his friend swallowed their drinks and walked out, but all the employees felt that they had been in danger. They sent for Harris, and one of his partners handed him a pistol as he approached the building. Thompson, unaware of the stir his presence had caused, met outside a friend who wished to eat, so together they walked back into the bar.

One of the employees saw Harris entering a moment later and whispered: 'Ben Thompson's here.'

Thompson heard people muttering that Jack had got his shotgun, and he saw through the swinging doors that Harris was standing behind the wall of the doorway with his gun resting on his crippled left hand, ready to shoot with his right.

Although at the trial later Thompson claimed that he cried out: 'Jack Harris, what are you doing with that gun?' and that Jack Harris had replied, adding some profanity: 'It's to shoot you,' that was too good a defence to be taken seriously after the event.

At any rate Thompson fired through the slats of the swinging door. The ball cut along the wall and passed into Harris near his heart. A second shot caught Harris as he fell, and a third was fired into the air to scare off any other conspirators. Thompson then stepped into the street among the hacks near the pavement, and he pointed his pistol at the band on the balcony. The musicians hurriedly went inside the building, and Thompson felt it was safe for him to turn his back and get away.

He went through several houses and over to the Menger Hotel, where he remained during the rest of that night and most of the next day. He was in considerable mental turmoil, but he finally decided to send for the sheriff and surrender. He allowed himself to be jailed in a comfortable room with iron bars at the windows. Then in a grandiose move of caring more for the reputation of his home town than for his own interests, he publicly resigned his job as Austin's marshal, pending his discharge.

The trial was held in January 1883 and lasted from Tuesday morning to Saturday night, with the courthouse crowded to capacity. The judge charged the jury at nightfall. At eight o'clock the next morning they brought in a verdict of 'not guilty'.

'At a reading of the verdict the applause was deafening and long continued,' reads a report of that time.

Freed at last, Thompson with his wife and daughter returned by train to Austin, where a crowd of people greeted him. Enthusiastic young men unharnessed the horses and drew his carriage by hand along the principal street, to celebrate his vindication.

Gradually Thompson had taken to drinking more and more heavily, and frequently he was the cause of disturbances in various parts of the city. Even when he shot off blank cartridges for fun scores of people who did not know he wasn't in earnest were frightened. He suffered from insomnia and liked to spend the nights roving from one quarter of the town to another, usually shooting playfully at anything he saw.

On March 10, 1884, Thompson met his old friend J. K. Fisher in Austin, and they spent several hours together. Late in the afternoon Fisher said he had to leave for Uvalde County, west of San Antonio, and he asked Thompson to go along with him. Reluctantly Thompson agreed to go part of the way, but it turned out that he stayed on the train as far as San Antonio. They arrived in that city, where Thompson had so frequently been in trouble, at about eight o'clock in the evening.

After several drinks the two went to the theatre to see *East Lynne*, and, following the eleven o'clock curtain, they wandered over to the Variety Theatre, where Jack Harris and his bartender had been killed. At the bar they met W. H. Sims, who was now running the place in partnership with Joe Foster. Thompson expressed a desire to see Foster so as to make friends with him again.

'The old trouble is all forgotten, you know,' said Thompson genially.

'Why don't you two go upstairs and watch the show?' said Sims.

While Thompson and Fisher were ordering drinks Sims joined them with Foster. Thompson lumbered to his feet and offered to shake hands, exclaiming: 'Foster, suppose we let bygones be bygones?'

It was characteristic of Ben Thompson, who usually dictated the terms of any relationship, that he should expect Foster to accept his overtures the moment he was inclined to be friendly, in spite of his repeated claims that Foster had tried to swindle him.

Foster backed away, unwilling to shake hands with the murderer of Jack Harris, a man he had admired. It may be that it seemed to Thompson that Foster reached for his gun as he jerked his hand away.

Regardless of the contradictory testimony at the coroner's inquest—the main object of which was to save anyone from prosecution—the fact remains that suddenly guns were fired. Joe Foster was hit in the leg. Thompson and Fisher, who had been standing at his right, both fell dead. It was found that Fisher was shot thirteen times. Thompson received nine bullets, five in his head and four in his body, all entering from the left. Any one of the head wounds would have been fatal.

Thus at forty-one Ben Thompson's career was ended by the same method he had used to conclude the lives of many men before him. But his single-minded attitude towards accomplishing his own purpose at any given moment, plus his uncanny courage, have established him in the annals of the West as a remarkable gunfighter, and an even more remarkable person.

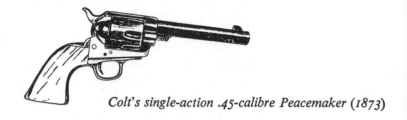

Colt's single-action .45-calibre Peacemaker (1873)

8 Clay Allison

CLAY ALLISON had the good fortune to live in the West during the nineteenth century. As far as can be ascertained, this was his only claim to fame. But he has been 'remembered' by many old-timers in search of a spot of glory for themselves as a man deserving a place in the history of the West. Not only avid collectors of rumours have become his enthusiastic biographers. Even careful research into contemporary newspaper accounts lead some writers—possibly unaware of the fallibility of small-town journalists—to assemble slight details into serious claims for the edification of posterity.

Nevertheless, the fact that only a few stories are left to us about Clay Allison's forty-seven-year career gives the impression that he was usually a well-behaved citizen. He was a successful cattle rancher and lived within his means and took his part in community life. He must have been respected. On one occasion he raised 10,000 dollars bail without trouble, in a location where he did not have property. His devotion to his brother is in his favour. When he faced trouble he transferred all his property to his brother's name, which shows that the family relationship was admirable.

It may have been his capability and his secure connections which produced in him a certain arrogance of manner. Certainly his wit led him into pranks which at times disturbed the peace.

At any rate, nothing evil is on Allison's record, his worst traits having appeared only when he was under the influence of alcohol.

And he lived during a period when every man considered himself under obligation to centre his social activities at the bars. Besides, the public lack of confidence in any established law bred men who took matters into their own hands when pressed.

There is agreement that Clay Allison—sometimes known as R. C. Allison—was born in Wayne County, Tennessee, in 1840 and died in Texas in 1887. Every place where he lived for any length of time claims the distinction of having been his residence. Northern New Mexico and Southern Colorado and the Texas Panhandle have all celebrated memories which may or may not have originated in his person. At least he is by now ensconced in 'colloquial history' to such an extent that any account of the West must take him into consideration.

Every man of character in those days and that region must have tangled with Wyatt Earp—or at least have it said he had. Even Clay Allison has such a rumour attached to his early life, though no extenuating circumstances are presented. However, the story goes that Bat Masterson had warned Clay Allison to steer clear of Dodge City. Since Clay took a dim view of such affronts, he said he would dispose of Masterson and then take over the town.

He invaded Dodge City one September dawn with ten trail-thirsty gunmen. At the Alhambra he stopped and yelled: 'Tell that Yankee-loving Masterson that Clay Allison is here.' His Southern drawl floated over the dusty street and echoed back in his ears. His riotous crew stormed up Front Street, hitting every bar. Fifty wild, yowling Texans trailed him into the Long Branch. Still no Masterson. Allison reeled outside and up to the Deadline, at the rail tracks.

South of the Deadline stood the saloons, dance-halls, brothels, and other dens of vice. But north of the tracks respectable citizens resided. To carry a weapon or raise your voice there meant being forcibly tossed into jail—or worse. But Allison staggered north! Behind him surged a drunken, cursing wave, six-shooters roaring to the accompaniment of tinkling glass and shrieks of unseen, terrified women.

The gunmen swaggered before the gunshop of Mayor 'Dog' Kelly, but that honourable sir failed to show himself. With a final burst of gunfire, and denouncing Bat Masterson, the drunken crowd returned to the Alhambra.

Yet the true story of Allison's invasion of Dodge City as told by eye-witnesses has a different hue. They claim he rode into town alone that morning and was not backed by any gang; that he had come to kill Wyatt Earp and not Masterson. Certain Texas cattlemen still fought the Lost Cause of the Confederacy and were weary of Yankee badge-toters in their state. Yet they feared to stand up against the fast-draw lawmen and had hired Allison's guns to do the work for them. They had promised to support Clay's actions in Dodge when and if a showdown came.

Bat Masterson was a deputy marshal of Dodge City at the time and had carried word to Wyatt as he breakfasted at the Dodge House.

'You'll need help this time, Wyatt,' he commented.

Earp calmly offered his deputy some coffee. 'Why? I believe I can take Allison.'

'Sure you can,' Bat agreed. 'But there's a dozen Texans hiding at Wright's place, and I aim to even the odds.'

While Earp continued eating he checked his Peacemaker, then left. Walking up Front Street to Second Avenue, he pretended to examine horse brands at the hitch-racks.

Wyatt stepped from the Dodge House and lit a cigar before strolling towards Second Avenue. Just as Earp neared the street, Allison turned the corner.

Both stopped warily and Allison asked: 'You Wyatt Earp?'

'I'm Earp,' admitted the marshal, cigar nudging his moustache.

Allison seemed confused. He flicked a glance at Wright's window, framing expectant Texan faces. Witnesses crowding batwing doors said he then bluntly accused Earp of killing his foreman, and began backing away.

'That's a lie,' Earp retorted honestly, and spat his cigar at Clay's boots. One hand hovered near his pistol butt, provocative and taunting.

There was a tense moment of utter silence. Then Allison went brick red beneath his tan. Growling something unintelligible to listeners, he turned and strode rapidly away. Earp just stood there. Shortly afterwards Allison rode from the livery stable. Spurs raking, he tore furiously up Front Street. Wyatt didn't move a muscle. At Wright's store Allison slid to a dust-clouded stop.

Clay Allison

'You sneaking coyotes!' he shouted angrily. 'A hell of a backing-up job you all did!' Reining about, he raced headlong out of town.

The cowardly cattlemen remained in hiding. Earp had one malevolent eye on the store window as he casually lit a fresh cigar. And across the street William Barclay Masterson lolled, grinning against a hitch-rail.

In a saloon in East St. Louis Allison was once supposed to have joined in a loud dispute with other drinkers. That also is a good possibility.

It is claimed that when a dentist in Cheyenne, or in Las Vegas, as some say, accidentally pulled the wrong tooth and thus failed to relieve his toothache, he wielded the pliers himself until he had removed all the dentist's good teeth. Nobody tells what the dentist was doing in the meantime, but it may be accepted that Clay Allison was gigantic and muscular.

He was six foot two and weighed twelve and a half stone. He had black hair and blue eyes, straight features excusing his pride in family, a determined mouth, and a bewhiskered chin. When sober he was quiet and unassuming, not at all the desperado type. He sat his saddle handsomely, and only when afoot displayed the limp which he usually tried to hide.

In his boyhood he had accidentally shot the instep of his right foot, and the injury was permanent. Even if he had not been surrounded by a gun-toting populace, that physical defect may have forced him to seek compensation in firearms and to take seriously any remarks which seemed to be veiled slights. But it was not unusual for a rancher of those days to be a crack shot, and no doubt Allison had practised with firearms for many years.

During the Civil War he enlisted in the Confederate Army. He was captured by Union soldiers and condemned to death as a spy. Before he could be executed he escaped. It was because his hands were unusually small that he was able to wriggle out of the handcuffs. It has been presumed that he killed a guard while making his getaway, but perhaps that is no more than a guess.

At the close of the war Allison became foreman for the cattlemen partners I. W. Lacy and L. G. Coleman, on Vermejo Creek, north of Cimarron, in Colfax County, New Mexico. Having learned the

157

business, he later ran his own herd with the brand of a Box Circle. He was accused of letting his cattle graze beyond his own pastures, south towards Fort Union and north to the ranges below Las Animas, Colorado, where he felt particularly at home.

Clay often joined friends at the bar of the Clifton House, which was on the Barlow and Sanderson Stage Line, and it was there that he shot and killed Chunk Tolbert. Chunk was buried on the hillside behind the Clifton House, where several impromptu graves had already been dug.

Although the Code of the West left Allison free when he explained that he had fired in self-defence, naturally the local inhabitants tried to discover a motive. Some explained that Chunk, having killed Walter Walled in a dance-hall near Trinidad, Colorado, made the mistake of coming to Las Animas. If Walled was a friend of Porter Stockton and Stockton was a friend of Allison, then Tolbert put himself in the way of chastisement by Allison's gun. On the other hand, some people said that Allison had once killed Chunk's uncle in a Texas knife-fight, and that Chunk had entered Allison's territory to avenge his uncle.

They met at Clifton House, had words, agreed to be reconciled, and seated themselves for a friendly meal together. Chunk's head was shot and dropped into his plate. Allison claimed that he shot only when he heard Chunk's gun touch the underside of the table as he tried to lift it for shooting across the board. Whether that was a figment of Allison's imagination or a well-groomed excuse, nobody will ever know.

The story goes that Allison's reputation as a ruthless gunman preceded him as he roamed from Trinidad to Las Animas and on to Pueblo. Though reports of men with guns always assure us of their courage, the obverse is always to the effect that residents of the area trembled with fear as though made of different clay. Yet, since Allison was a heavy drinker, there may have been reason for people to keep their children off the streets when he was abroad.

Whenever he rode down the main street shouting for somebody to put out the lights, then rode back shooting out the lights which had not been extinguished, he was in his cups—but not sufficiently to alert the authorities. At least, the officers did not make an attempt to arrest him. They explained that he never did get drunk enough to hurt anybody. Evidently they were not willing to test this theory; he might have damaged them before they could prove it.

Once in Rufe Harrington's New State Saloon at El Moro, north of Trinidad, Allison had an argument with Buckskin Charlie and beat him up, so that Charlie had to be taken to hospital. The reason for the fracas was not reported.

Another time Allison shot holes through Dr. Menger's hat and then bought him a new one, companionably buying him a drink at the same time.

On still another evening Allison commanded everybody in a saloon to dance, and trained his guns on their feet. One young fellow managed to slip out of the door unnoticed, and he returned at the other door—behind Allison. Then the tables were turned and Allison himself had to dance. When this assailant tried to duck out while still covering Allison, the latter hailed him to come back and be friends.

'You've got good stuff in you,' Allison called to him, 'and we need men like you in this country.'

The Federal Government rejected the claim of the Maxwell Land Grant and Railway Company to a strip of two million acres, and there was naturally a sudden influx of new settlers. The cattlemen found the range threatened even more than ever, and they organized themselves into the Industrial Association of New Mexico. Clay Allison was on the rules committee.

By 1875 the homesteaders were ploughing and driving strange cattle off their acreage. In a number of cases they killed the marauding cows who refused to leave. Warrants were sworn out for the settlers who had dared to destroy the property of the ranchers.

Trial was at first set for May 4 in Cimarron, but there was one postponement after another. The settlers were held in suspense, until they appealed to Clay Allison to help them. Allison is supposed to have threatened Ernest, the most vindictive of the ranchers. Ernest left town, never to return. After that the case was held over for the following autumn, but it was never called. Since Allison was a member of the Stockgrowers' Association, it seems surprising that he sided with the homesteaders. But it is conceivable that he considered them in the right and acted on his own. He was always able to think for himself.

Bennington DuPont was an Easterner staying at the Wright House in Dodge City, and he made an unfavourable impression. He was nicknamed the Ground Owl, 'because,' Cimarron Bill said, 'rattlesnakes don't kill ground owls and nobody knows wherefore'.

When Clay Allison, on a cattle-buying errand from Las Animas, stopped at the Wright House for a drink, he wanted a doughnut from the free-lunch bowl. He asked the next man at the brass rail, who happened to be the Ground Owl: 'Pard, please pass the fried holes.'

The Ground Owl had watched Allison limp into the bar-room, and now he accepted this remark as a second point to evoke his laughter.

'Say,' he said. 'You limp in your talk like you do in your walk.'

Allison, as usual sensitive about his injured foot, put his Colt up to the stranger's scarred face.

In terror the Ground Owl cried: 'Don't shoot. I ain't armed.'

'Go heel yourself, varmint,' said Allison. 'I'm waitin'.'

The Ground Owl ran into a stack of alfalfa behind the Trask corral, and after dark he got away with his skin.

That was the day when Bat Masterson, the sheriff, thought he was going to have to stop Allison with his own gun. But, as Allison afterwards claimed, he had a premonition that there would be trouble if he happened to touch his guns while walking along the main street of Dodge. He took the first opportunity to tell his side of the story about the Ground Owl, and Masterson agreed that he had done the right thing to relieve Dodge of that disagreeable character.

But every Goliath has his David, and Allison was no exception.

A churlish young gunslinger named Buck Bowman returned to his home range during Cimarron's annual Mexican fiesta. Strutting about and flaunting twelve notches on his pistol-butt, he quickly cowed the local talent.

Pushing his luck, he noisily bragged: 'I hear some Johnny Reb named Allison is top-gun hereabouts. I aim to make him thirteen on my pistol handle.'

One of Clay's riders overheard. Shortly the entire gang was in town. But Clay was alone when he saw Buck emerging from Yee Fong's steak-house.

'You Bowman?' he accosted him. The hard-faced, black-garbed

160

youth answered his rider's description, but he had to be certain. Not even Clay Allison could gun down some rancher's son in a fiesta crowd and laugh it off. The merrymakers outnumbered his men—and lynch mobs formed fast.

Buck's lip curled as he shoved back his hat.

'Sure am, hombre, and what of it?'

'I'm Allison,' Clay drawled in his Southern brogue. 'I hear you-all got a big mouth.'

He backed off five short steps. Then Bowman crouched, his elbows crooked, and both clawed hands streaked for leather. Allison's gun hand blurred—the big Navy Colt bucked and roared. The heavy wallop of the .45 slug spun Bowman clear round. His guns spanged a vicious echo, and dust sprayed Clay's boots. But it was the reflex act of a dead man.

For once nobody blamed Clay. Folks agreed Buck got what he had asked for. And Clay got looped, unaware that he had fixed to meet his 'David'.

Monday evening a burly stockman with drooping moustaches rode up to the Otero ranch-house and was invited to supper. Afterwards he announced he was Mason B. Bowman of the Rocking-B spread, down near Tres Ritos.

'I'm Buck's uncle,' he said quietly, 'and I aim to even the score, but being a fair-minded man I'll hear your side first.'

Clay's face was impassive as he offered the rancher a drink. Mase Bowman was a man of ominous repute. As a gun-swift lawman of the Texas Ranger McNelly calibre, he had made cowtown Tascosa unhealthy for characters like Allison until turning rancher. And Tascosa was Dodge and Tombstone and Abilene tied together on a short, lighted fuse.

Clay Allison explained how Buck had forced the shoot-out.

Bowman listened. 'Buck did have a mean streak in him. I suppose it was you or him.' They drank and discussed calf crops until bedtime.

It should have ended so. But Clay awoke feeling he had been insulted. To his neurotic mind, Bowman would depart thinking he had feared a showdown. During breakfast he dropped sarcastic remarks about 'has-been' lawmen.

'I'm warning you, Allison, take care. I'm no trigger-happy kid like Buck. Draw and you're dead.'

Clay's features twisted in silent rage. But he did not draw and he let no rider interfere. His brothers were gone, having moved to Colorado. To save face he pretended that he had been joking, and said he would accompany Mase to Cimarron. Mase agreed. Knowing gunslingers, he rode behind.

As they dismounted before Lambert's, Clay swiftly drew his pistol, but Bowman had his Walker Colt levelled and cocked before he could use it. Clay sheepishly led the way inside. There he tried again and met Mase's icy, mocking grin across a .44's sights. Yet Mase did not pull the trigger. It seemed he enjoyed humiliating Clay before the other patrons.

Livid with rage, Allison tried to get Bowman intoxicated. Several times Clay drew his pistol and managed to equal Mase's fast draw several times; but Bowman's taunting grin said he'd get him anyway.

Bowman even out-drank Allison, who finally passed out cold. Amazed but joyful patrons loaded him on to his pony and headed it homeward.

In the autumn of 1875 a murder took place somewhere between Taos and Cimarron. It excited Allison's anger and inspired many efforts on his part to apprehend the culprit.

The Rev. F. J. Tolby, a Methodist, having held his usual Sunday church service at the mining camp called Elizabethtown, on Monday or Tuesday rode back over the twenty miles to Cimarron. On the way he was shot through the heart.

Since he was not robbed, and since his horse was neatly tied to a tree not far from the body, the crime was baffling. The Rev. O. P. McMains wanted to clear up the mystery. He carried Tolby's blood-spattered saddle around with him, showing it to everybody and urging that something be done.

It was known that Tolby had written a letter to the *New York Sun* opposing the Santa Fe Ring, which controlled elections and appointments in the New Mexico territorial government. The first suspicion was against the Ring, and for several weeks Allison hunted for clues.

Finally Cruz Vega was implicated. On the night of October 30, 1875, a mob dragged him from his hut and hanged him from a telegraph pole. He was forced to confess before he was left dangling, and he insisted that the gun which killed Tolby had been fired by

Manuel Cardenas. The arrest of Cardenas followed. While he was being led to jail he was shot through the head by a group of self-appointed deputy sheriffs.

For the purpose of avenging his friend Cruz Vega, Francisco (Pancho) Griego rode into Cimarron, declaring that he was after Clay Allison, whom he considered the leader of the two lynch mobs. At the bar in Henry Lambert's St. James Hotel Allison gratified the stranger's desire by striding up to him and asking: 'Lookin' for me?'

The two of them withdrew to a corner in order to talk. Suddenly three shots sounded, and Griego fell. Somebody had the presence of mind to extinguish the lights, and the body was left lying there till morning.

No charge was ever made against Allison, and it was taken for granted that he had shot in self-defence, as so often before.

This incident may have been the pivot on which the policy of the *Cimarron News and Press* turned. Until then the columns of that local paper had been lauding Allison for his civic pride in searching for the murderer of the Rev. Tolby. Now, however, one of the owners of the paper, William D. Dawson, began to side with the Santa Fe Ring and to comment on Allison's recklessness with a gun. He received several warnings to desist, but he continued his crusade.

On the night of January 18, 1876, a mob entered Dawson's office and threw his presses into the river. Clay Allison found that the first page of the January 22 issue had already been printed, but the reverse side was still blank. He ran on the blank page in red letters: CLAY ALLISON'S EDITION. Then he sold copies for twenty-five cents apiece as he strolled up and down the main street.

Years later somebody said that as soon as Allison had sobered up he returned to the newspaper office and voluntarily paid two hundred dollars towards the cost of the damage.

Still in Cimarron, Allison was drinking in Lambert's saloon on March 24 when three Negro soldiers from Captain Moore's detachment entered through the swinging doors. All three were suddenly shot to death before they had quite crossed the threshold. Clay Allison did not deny that he was the one who had aired his Southern sympathies in this way.

Although many such deaths were left uninvestigated, in this case the dead Negroes had been Federal soldiers, and an attempt was made to name their murderer. One report ran that the murderer was a certain Davy Crockett[1] who had been a drinking companion of Allison at the time, and that Crockett was killed the following day by Deputy Sheriff Joe Holbrook while trying to escape town. But Holbrook's shooting of Crockett actually occurred a year and a half later, in September 1877.

There was no law in Cimarron at that time. A lesser man than Captain Francis Dodge might have gone off half cocked when he heard of the murder of his three troopers. In fact, his remaining twenty troopers angrily clamoured for permission to ride out to the Allison ranch, near Otero, to exact revenge.

Dodge refused. His fury was, however, no less because it was controlled. He sent a courier to Taos for the sheriff. The trooper returned alone. The wily lawman wanted no part of the dreaded Texas Allisons. But he did send a warrant. If Dodge brought Clay in, then he would see that the gunslinger stood trial.

At noon the following day Dodge rode up to the Allison ranch-house, with two sets-of-fours as escorts. Boldly he approached the porch.

'Clay Allison!' he called. 'I have a warrant for your arrest!'

The door creaked open, and the barrel of a Green shotgun appeared. Behind it came Allison, sneering.

Ignoring Dodge, he waved the wicked-looking shotgun at the mounted troopers. 'You all got ten seconds to hightail it for town.'

'See here, now,' protested Captain Dodge, brandishing the warrant.

'Don't wave that paper at me, Captain.' Shotgun hammers clicked ominously. Allison's face reflected the cruelty and ferocity of which he was capable and for which he was widely noted.

Captain Dodge was no coward. His record in the Indian wars bore that out. Nor was he a fool. Side-glances revealed semi-hidden gunmen ready to bear down on the visitors at the first hostile move. To prevent further slaughter, he ordered the eight fuming troopers to leave.

'I'll ride into town with you, Captain, but I aim to wear my guns,' said Clay.

[1] This Davy Crockett was no relation of the famous frontiersman, Davy Crockett, who was killed at the Battle of the Alamo in Texas, 1836.

Dodge did not press the issue.

Cimarron must have gaped when the pair rode in with Allison still armed. Even now it seems incredible. But that wasn't all. Allison insisted they have a drink at the bar, and Dodge prudently posted sentries outside Lambert's. When the sheriff arrived he expected to see Allison in irons as Dodge had promised him. The lawman had thought that with his troopers Dodge could easily subdue Allison. Captain Dodge turned Clay over to the sheriff with the 'prisoner' still wearing his guns.

Clay Allison was arrested on March 30, a week after the saloon shooting, and he was taken to Taos by Sheriff Rinehart with a detachment of soldiers. This may have been merely a gesture to satisfy the Army, however, for Allison was soon released. The sheriff's excuse was that Allison had managed to get behind a rock and raised a gun on the detachment, which scattered.

In December of that year Allison was once more in the news, this time in Las Animas. He and his brother John were at the Olympic Dance Hall, wearing their guns on the floor. Charles Faber, the constable, asked them to conform to the rules by leaving their arms outside. They refused to comply.

Faber withdrew to the American Hotel and secured a double-barrelled Green 10-gauge shotgun from Tom Gartrell, the night clerk. He appointed two citizens who were idling nearby to be his deputies, and with them he returned to the dance-hall, meaning to enforce his cordial request to the Allisons.

Although every charge of shooting against Clay Allison was accompanied by a claim that someone else shot first, it may be discounted in this case. Faber had the law on his side and deputies with him. He no doubt did aim his shotgun at John Allison—not knowing which was Clay, some explain—but it is doubtful that he fired first. However, Clay saw the manœuvre and shot Faber before he had entered the doorway. If Faber had not already shot John, he did so then, but he fell dead on the doorstep immediately afterwards, and his deputies vanished. They had been reluctant to accompany him in the first place, and they didn't want anybody to learn their identities.

John was severely wounded. While he was being carried to the Vandiver House, where the brothers had rooms, Clay made it clear to his wounded brother that his assailant had been killed. He seemed to take comfort from being able to assure John that vengeance had been swift.

Within a few days Sheriff Spiers arrested both the Allisons and took them to the new stone jail in Las Animas. Justice of the Peace John M. Jay presided at the preliminary hearing, and ordered Clay to be committed to jail to await the action of the grand jury. John Allison was moved to the nearest hospital.

On January 6, 1877, Clay was brought before District Judge John W. Henry in Pueblo on a writ of *habeas corpus* which his attorney, Thomas Macon, presented on his behalf. Accusing Clay of manslaughter, the judge set bail at 10,000 dollars, and that amount was obtained immediately.

On February 3, when John Allison was presumed sufficiently recovered to stand trial, Judge Jay discharged him for lack of evidence, and Clay took him back to Cimarron. Clay may have been doubtful about the coming decision of the grand jury. At least, he transferred all his belongings in Colfax County to his brother's name.

However, when the court adjourned on March 29 'no bill was found against R. C. Allison'. Again Clay's claim of self-defence had freed him.

In 1881, when he was settled in Washita, not far from Mobeetie, in Hemphill County, Texas, Clay married Dora McCullough. They bought a ranch in the Seven Rivers area of Southern New Mexico.

It is said that Clay was one day dining at the Wright Hotel in Dodge City when a Mexican who had threatened his life walked into the dining-room with gun in hand. Allison shot him in the centre of the forehead, killing him instantly, and then resumed eating his meal without rising from his chair.

Thereupon the marshal reminded him that there was a new regulation that all men entering the city should be disarmed. He asked Clay to surrender his guns. When Clay politely declined, the marshal stepped up with some deputies in order to disarm him.

'Gentlemen,' said Clay calmly, 'when these pistols go off they go off smoking.'

The marshal retreated after Clay had agreed to keep the peace until he had made his necessary purchases and had left Dodge City.

Clay was a member of the first grand jury ever appointed in

Hemphill County. Although the foreman kept the jury together for twenty-eight days, all of the jurors were too tipsy to turn in any indictment to the court. Clay Allison especially was hilarious the whole term.

About this time rustling on the Washita became a worse menace than usual, and the cattlemen called for a meeting one night to discuss what could be done to remedy the situation.

Clay Allison said coolly: 'Do you really want to know who the damned thieves are?'

'Yes!'

'Well,' said Allison, 'two of them are sitting among us. There they are!'

The two men he pointed out pulled their guns and leaped for the doorway. They dashed round the corner of the house.

'Look out, Allison, or they'll shoot you through the window!' cried somebody.

With both pistols drawn, Allison stood in the corner of the room and bellowed: 'Come back here, you calf-stealing hypocrites.'

The guilty men were never again seen in that area.

From that time on Clay Allison attended to his own business and enjoyed life with his family while he raised cattle.

In July 1887 he was at the home of a friend who had already loaded a freight wagon with two teams hitched for a long haul. In a spirit of fun Clay climbed to the driver's board and cracked a whip over the horses and let out a yip. He was known to be an outstandingly good handler of horses.

As the team started up, the wagon struck a chuck-hole, and Allison was thrown down between the wheels. The rear wheel of the heavily loaded wagon ran over him, breaking his back and his neck.

His dare-devil days were over.

But the old-timers still spin yarns about him. Almost every move he made has inspired talk that has become more and more colourful with the passage of time.

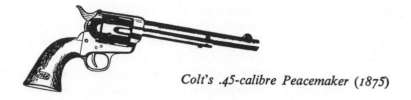

Colt's .45-calibre Peacemaker (1875)

9 Frank Leslie

BILLY CLAIBORNE was nasty drunk as he shouldered apart the swinging doors of the Oriental Saloon that chilly morning of November 19, 1882. As his mean bloodshot eyes darted about he smirked arrogantly. Four notches on his .45 butt made him fancy himself another Billy the Kid. Some of his outlaw friends jokingly called him that just to see him strut. Had the real Kid still been alive Billy Claiborne would not have dared to use the sobriquet. Nor did Billy awe the elite gunmen of Tombstone as he tried to act tough. The young braggart had never faced a top-gun. Few believed he would after his cowardly flight from the O.K. Corral fiasco.

It was shortly after seven. A lone miner was conversing with Frank Leslie, the bartender. Otherwise the Oriental was deserted.

Swaggering up to the bar, Claiborne ordered whisky.

Leslie's drooping blond moustache twisted in a pleasant grin.

'I'd say you've had enough already, Billy.'

Claiborne pounded the bar. 'To hell with you. Give me some whisky and quick.'

'You're drunk, Billy. Best go sober up,' advised Leslie.

Billy Claiborne left the saloon, but once outside he felt that he had been grossly insulted, and decided he had a score to settle with 'Buckskin' Frank Leslie, the bartender. Billy had been on good terms with Leslie when the body of John Ringo, noted Tombstone gunslinger, was discovered in suspicious circumstances that pointed to Leslie. Ringo's death preyed upon Billy's mind. As a friend of

Frank Leslie

Ringo, he felt that it was up to him to avenge his death by putting Leslie out of circulation. Others claimed that Billy's egomania caused him to 'commit suicide' by tangling with gunman Leslie.

Billy returned to the Oriental. Staring bleary-eyed at Leslie, he proclaimed in a loud voice: 'You can't insult me like this, Leslie.'

Frank Leslie then left the bar, and, seizing Billy by the coat collar, pushed him through the door and into the street.

Half an hour later word was brought to Leslie that Billy Claiborne was back, and standing outside the front door, armed with a Winchester rifle and blustering in drunken abandonment that he was there to kill the bartender. Leslie simply shrugged his shoulders as he waited on his customers. Many figured that Claiborne was just 'shooting off his mouth' and would not dare to tackle Leslie. Leslie was of the elite. Some even ranked him a shade faster than Doc Holliday—though he wasn't a deadly killer like Doc.

When patrons began kidding Leslie about the braggart at the door he replied: 'Well, Billy and I have been good friends. I'll just go see what he's spouting about.'

Leslie leisurely removed his white apron and then opened a drawer behind the bar, picked out his six-gun, and walked to a side-door leading into Fifth Street.

Billy Claiborne stood on the corner of Allen Street, his rifle cradled in his arms. Leslie silently approached him. When only about thirty feet from the drunken youth, he covered him with his six-gun and called: 'Billy!'

The young cowboy swung about, and when he saw Leslie threw his rifle to his shoulder and pulled the trigger. Billy's rifle and Frank's pistol fired almost simultaneously, but Billy missed, while Leslie's slug struck Billy in the chest, and he collapsed.

As onlookers poured into the street, one guffawed: 'He shore warn't no Billy the Kid. Missed with a saddle-gun at thirty feet.'

Leslie didn't join them. Turning about, he returned to the Oriental and placed his revolver in the drawer. Tying his apron around him, he turned to a customer and asked: 'What's yours, partner?'

Billy Claiborne passed away within an hour. Meanwhile, Leslie went about his work as unconcerned as if he had just swatted

169

a mosquito instead of a former pal. Leslie was given a hearing, but was acquitted on a claim and proof of self-defence.

This was Tombstone in its heyday. Born of danger and necessity in June 1879, on an arid Arizona mesa called Goose Flats, it had been named by its founder, Ed Schieffelin, an old Army Scout whose discovery of fabulous silver-mines brought thousands of miners and gunmen into the territory.

United States Army Scout Al Sieber had warned Schieffelin that he would not find gold in the San Pedro Valley, but would find his tombstone instead.

'That's Geronimo County, Ed, and filled with Apaches,' Sieber had told him.

Yet Ed refused to listen. He knew the danger when he rode his mule into those low, forbidding, almost naked hills in 1877. Ed was careful and ambitious. He found the mountain of silver from which was spawned the town of Tombstone.

Word of the fabulous riches to be mined in the hills spread. Men from every station of life flocked into the district, and the new town of Tombstone grew up. Ed Schieffelin lived in luxury and later travelled all over the world. He eventually tired of civilization and left his palatial Los Angeles home for a trip into the wilds of Oregon, to enjoy the freedoms of an outdoor man. There he suffered a stroke and died surrounded by loneliness.

His remains were shipped back to Tombstone. There he was laid to rest, dressed in a miner's corduroy breeches and red flannel shirt, and his old pick, shovel, and canteen were placed beside him in his coffin. A huge miners' monument of rough stone was erected to mark his last resting-place.

And into Tombstone rode Frank Leslie. The claim staked by Leslie was rich in ore and would probably have made him a rich man, but he disliked work, and left his mine to be run by hired help, while he devoted his time to the lustful glamour of the painted Junos and the lure of the card games.

Frank's neglect of his mine proved disastrous. One day he found that it had been annexed to the holdings of one of the powerful combines. He took court action only to learn that a legal technicality had been found, and his holdings were lawfully the property of the big interests.

The loss of his mine appeared to have no effect on Leslie's way of life. He was a good gambler and took his loss with a grin. There were other ways of making money without too much effort, so he took up the vocation of a gambler. Luck smiled on his efforts, and he soon acquired enough capital to continue his easy-going ways.

No more romantic figure ever graced the town of Tombstone than jovial, boisterous Leslie, garbed in his Kit Carson rig. Handsome, with long blond hair falling to his buckskin-clad shoulders, a pair of six-guns draping his lean hips, he created a furore among the weaker sex, and drew speculative glances from the male population as he swaggered through the streets. Many called him the buckskin-clad Adonis of Tombstone; others tagged the new arrival as just some 'ham' actor displaying his wardrobe. Later they learned their mistake, for concealed by his fetching smile and flamboyant dress was a vindictive, passionate nature. He was a gunman who could back his play with one of the fastest draws in the district. He demonstrated as much by killing some of Tombstone's citizens.

Weary of the attention bestowed upon him by the damsels to be found in his usual haunts, Frank Leslie sought new faces elsewhere. One night at a dance he met an enchanting woman named Mrs. Mary Killeen. She was a raven-haired, blue-eyed beauty who had recently separated from her husband, Michael Killeen, an employee at the Crystal Palace, where he acted as lookout and bouncer.

Frank Leslie fell hard for this woman, and she responded to his amorous attentions. The dance over, Leslie escorted his new partner to the Commercial Hotel, where Mrs. Killeen had taken a room after separating from her husband. Word reached Mike Killeen that his wife and Leslie were attending dances together. Mrs. Killeen feared the wrath of her husband, but she still continued to meet Frank Leslie. The husband became unable to control his jealousy. He left the Crystal Palace and took up a station near the hotel, to await the return of his wife.

Men might hate Leslie, but no man scorned him. He was too dangerous. Mike Killeen took a chance on Leslie's gun and temper, and confronted his wife and her escort. There were words, and Killeen took a shot at Leslie. He missed. It was a mistake to miss in those days. Frank made a smooth, fast draw and sent a slug crashing into Killeen's head. Holstering his six-gun, Leslie again took Mrs.

Killeen's arm, and without a second look at his victim led her into the hotel. None of the bystanders interfered. Such was Tombstone and such was Frank Leslie during the roaring 'eighties. Mike Killeen had openly threatened to kill Leslie, who had defended his life, so no legal action followed the shooting.

Within a few weeks Mary Killeen and the forty-year-old Frank Leslie were married and rented a cottage. Frank, however, proved to be a husband who could not content himself with devoting all his time to one woman, and the marriage went on the rocks. Mary Leslie divorced him, and later married Alexander Derwood. The newly-weds left Tombstone for California, and were never heard of again.

Frank Leslie, once more a bachelor, became a bartender in the Oriental Saloon owned by Mike Joice. The upper floor of the building was devoted to gambling operated by Lou Rickabaugh and associates, one of whom was Wyatt Earp. Leslie and Earp met at various times, but Frank kept himself neutral, and when the clash finally came between the Earp and Behan factions he was not dragged into the affair. Leslie was too crafty to mix his play with others, and always played a lone-wolf game.

But the day dawned when the wild days of Tombstone were over. The battle of the O.K. Corral touched off the spark which brought the Earp-Behan feud to a head. Earp and his cohorts left Tombstone on March 21, 1882, and later Sheriff Johnny Behan was removed from office. The middle 'eighties saw the mines flooded and an exodus of citizens, until only a few hundred remained in Tombstone. Among those who left was Frank Leslie. He rejoined the Apache Scouts and remained with Gatewood until the surrender of Geronimo. Later he returned to his old stomping-grounds, and then took to drinking heavily. During one of his bouts he announced to some cronies: 'I'm getting tired of being alone. Reckon I'll get married.'

Not long afterwards he proposed to Diamond Annie, a 'red light' matron. She accepted him, and they were married. He and his bride drove to his ranch in the Whitestone Mountains, where they set up housekeeping. With them they took a seventeen-year-old youth who had drifted into Tombstone. He had no home, and Annie insisted that Leslie take him along to do the chores about the ranch.

Leslie became jealous of the attentions bestowed on the youth by his wife. Returning from town one day, and well liquored up, his homicidal nature asserted itself when he saw the boy leave the house.

With an oath, Frank Leslie sunk spurs to his horse and dashed into the yard. Drawing his pistol, he sent a slug towards the boy, who fell in a heap and lay still. The blast of the gun brought Mrs. Leslie rushing outside.

'Damn you, Leslie,' she cried, 'why did you shoot the boy? He never did a thing.'

Up came Leslie's pistol as he shouted: 'Here's a pill for you too, you no-good bastard!' The pistol roared again, and the slug struck Mrs. Leslie in the head, killing her instantly.

His passion satisfied, Leslie reined his horse round and headed back for Tombstone. No sooner had he ridden out of sight of the ranch than the inert figure of the boy came to life. The boy, named Jimmy Hibbs by some and Jim Hughes by others, was not harmed. When Leslie's bullet missed him he realized that by playing 'possum' he would probably be safe. He hurried to the corral, caught a horse, and took a wide detour at a fast clip, which enabled him to reach town ahead of Leslie. He went at once to the sheriff's office and explained what had happened. The boy was placed in another room until Leslie's arrival. Before long Leslie called at the sheriff's office.

'Get up a posse quick, Sheriff! The damned Injuns just killed my wife and hired hand,' he told them.

Leslie then gave a graphic story of how he had made the gruesome discovery of the two dead bodies lying in his ranch-yard when he reached home. The officer listened attentively.

'Take it easy. I'll soon have the guilty party in jail,' the sheriff stated.

Deceived by the man's attitude, Leslie turned and started for the door, then halted as he felt the muzzle of a gun pressing hard against his spine. A harsh voice ordered him to elevate his hands.

'What in hell is the meaning of this?' gaped the surprised Leslie.

'I'll show you,' replied the officer, and then called the boy into the room.

At sight of his supposed victim the killer's spirit broke. He realized his plan had failed. Leslie readily admitted that he had shot and killed his wife. Tried for this deed, he was found guilty and sentenced to serve twenty-five years in the State Penitentiary at Yuma.

Leslie was received at Yuma on December 10, 1889, and booked as Convict 632, height five feet, seven and one quarter inches, weight five pounds under ten stone. When it came time for outfitting the prisoner in convict garb, it was found impossible to find shoes to fit his small feet, so Leslie was permitted to retain his own size-five boots. He was also given the privilege of retaining his luxuriant moustache instead of being clean-shaven, as was the.prison rule. Frank Leslie found he was not the only former resident of Tombstone in the Yuma prison when he met Johnny Behan. Behan, however, was not serving time. He was the prison superintendent.

Frank Leslie proved himself a model prisoner, and was soon made a 'trusty'. Four years later he was instrumental in preventing a prison break. His action saved the lives of several prison guards, and for his services he was rewarded with a pardon. In 1893 he was released.

Once again a free man, Frank Leslie headed for Mexico, where he found employment in the mines. Later he returned to the States, and in California married a woman who had befriended him while his pardon was being considered. In 1896 he headed for the Klondike goldfields. It was reported he made a small fortune there, and then disappeared from the public eye.

In the middle 1930's the writer and a friend drifted into Ely, Nevada, and while in a saloon were waited on by a middle-aged bartender, a friendly person with a flare for conversation.

'Strangers in town?' he asked.

'Just riding through,' I replied.

'It's a wide-open town, but not like some I've been in,' said the bartender.

'Such as?' we naturally wanted to know.

'Well, Tombstone, for instance. It was a real tough town in its day.'

'You there when such characters as Frank Leslie and Wyatt Earp were around?' we asked.

'Yes, I was there. Funny thing about Leslie. After he was released from prison he disappeared, and I saw him only once after that. I was tending bar in Oakland, California, when an old derelict drifted into the place and asked the boss for a job. He was such a pathetic-looking old man that the boss took him on as a swamper. Somehow he reminded me of someone I had met before, but it wasn't until the next day that I realized who he was. He was Frank Leslie.'

'I don't see how you could recognize him after all those years,' I said.

A strange look was mirrored on the man's face as he said: 'How could I remember? A man doesn't forget someone who tried to kill him. I was the boy who worked for Leslie on his ranch when he killed his wife!'

It is true that Leslie found his way to California and took a job sweeping and cleaning up in a combination saloon and pool-hall. He did not remain long, however, and when he left he took with him the owner's revolver. That was in 1924.

What really became of the once swashbuckling Buckskin Frank Leslie is a moot question. In 1948 a decrepit man was admitted to the hospital in San Diego, California, under the name of Barney McCoy. He appeared to be around ninety years old. Shortly afterwards the old man passed away, but before he died he stated that his real name was Frank Leslie. It might have been, for Frank would have been in his nineties at that time. He was born during the 1850's. The exact date is unknown.

As for Tombstone, it grew and prospered. It is much today as it was in the past, minus the old-time violence. The O.K. Corral was made into a garage, the Birdcage Theatre into a cocktail lounge and museum, and the Alhambra into a grocer's. Although stricken several times by fire and floods, the town cannot die—not so long as the ghosts of Earp, Leslie, Behan, the Clantons, Curly Bill, Johnny Ringo, and other old gunfighters stalk shoulder-to-shoulder down Fremont Street.

The Gunfighter: Epilogue

Gunfighter! Gunfighter! Where do you roam?
    Always on the loose, no place to call home.
Dusty and forlorn; with not much pride;
    Two forty-fours hanging at your side.
Hitting the trail be it night or day,
    Looking for a fight to come your way.

From the Dakotas down to the Rio Grande
    You'll welcome a draw from any man.
Maybe you're right; maybe you're wrong;
    But your gun is fast and your will strong.
You ride into town so easy and slow—
    People gaze upon you—they want to know—

Where do you come from, who might you be?
    Just a tough gunfighter trying to stay free—
A time will come, perhaps you'll lose or win,
    Someone may be faster and check your guns in.
When the last fight is over and dust settles at your feet,
    It'll be too late, Mr. Gunfighter, will anyone weep?

C. W. B.